Criminalization of Politics

Criminalization of Politics

Marko Nikolić

SOCIETY Publishing

www.societypublishing.com

Criminalization of Politics

Marko Nikolić

Society Publishing
224 Shoreacres Road
Burlington, ON L7L 2H2
Canada
www.societypublishing.com
Email: orders@arclereducation.com

ISBN: 978-1-77407-794-8 (Hardcover)

ABOUT THE AUTHOR

Marko obtained his Master's degree from University of Belgrade - Faculty of Law in 2014. He specialized in Criminal Law, Family Law and Environmental Law. He spent his Master year studying about international child abduction. He was employed in Ministry of Defense's Legal Department and was also working as a legal secretary in numerous educational institutions. His freelance engagements are including more than 30 long-term clients. In addition to professional literature, he published a novel on the subject of history and mythology.

TABLE OF CONTENTS

GLOSSARY

A

Adherence – attachment or commitment to a person, cause, or belief.

Anthropologists – an anthropologist is a person engaged in the practice of anthropology. Anthropology is the study of aspects of humans within past and present societies.

Authoritative – proceeding from an official source and requiring compliance or obedience.

Autogenic – self-generated.

B

Bailiff – a sheriff's officer who executes writs and processes and carries out distraints and arrests.

Ballot – a system of voting secretly and in writing on a particular issue.

Bandwagon – Used in reference to an activity, cause, etc. that is currently fashionable or popular and attracting increasing support.

C

Clientelism – a social order which depends on relations of patronage.

Conniving – given to or involved in conspiring to do something immoral, illegal, or harmful.

Convicted – having been declared guilty of a criminal offense by the verdict of a jury or the decision of a judge.

D

De facto – existing or holding a specified position in fact but not necessarily by legal right.

Delegated – entrust (a task or responsibility) to another person, typically one who is less senior than oneself.

Derogatory – showing a critical or disrespectful attitude.

Disparaging – expressing the opinion that something is of little worth; derogatory.

E

Enactment – the process of passing legislation.

Endogeneity – situations in which an explanatory variable is correlated with the error term.

F

Femininity – qualities or Attributes Regarded as Characteristic of Women.

Fiduciary – involving trust, especially with regard to the relationship between a trustee and a beneficiary.

Fungible – (of goods contracted for without an individual specimen being specified) replaceable by another identical item; mutually interchangeable.

G

Gangdom – gangs or gangsters collectively; the world of organized crime, the criminal underworld.

Genocide – the deliberate killing of a large group of people, especially those of a particular nation or ethnic group.

H

Heterosexual – sexually attracted to people of the opposite sex.

I

Ideological – based on or relating to a system of ideas and ideals, especially concerning economic or political theory and policy.

Incumbent – necessary for (someone) as a duty or responsibility.

Inheritance – property passing at the owner's death to the heir or those entitled to succeed.

Interwoven – blend closely.

Intrusive – causing disruption or annoyance through being unwelcome or uninvited.

J

Jeopardized – put (someone or something) into a situation in which there is a danger of loss, harm, or failure.

L

Lobbyists – a person who takes part in an organized attempt to influence legislators.

M

Masculinity – qualities or attributes regarded as characteristic of men.

Matrifocal – based on the mother as the head of the family or household.

Matrilineal – of or based on kinship with the mother or the female line.

O

Oblivious – not aware of or concerned about what is happening around one.

Ostracism – exclusion from a society or group.

P

Patronage – the power to control appointments to office or the right to privileges.

Pervasiveness – the quality of spreading widely or being present throughout an area or a group of people.

Polyandry – it is a form of polygamy in which a woman takes two or more husbands at the same time.

Polygyny – it is a form of polygamy, involving one male and two or more females.

Protocol – the official procedure or system of rules governing affairs of state or diplomatic occasions.

R

Retribution – punishment inflicted on someone as vengeance for a wrong or criminal act.

Revocation – the official cancellation of a decree, decision, or promise.

S

Skepticism – a skeptical attitude; doubt as to the truth of something.

Stringent – (of regulations, requirements, or conditions) strict, precise, and exacting.

T

Taxonomic – concerned with the classification of things, especially organisms.

V

Varicolored – consisting of several different colors.

LIST OF FIGURES

LIST OF TABLES

LIST OF ABBREVIATIONS

ACOBOL	Association of Councilors of Bolivia
AFD	Alternative for Germany
ICC	International Criminal Court
ILO	International Labor Organization
IMF	International Monetary Fund
IPU	Interparliamentary Union
OHCHR	Office of the High Commissioner for Human Rights
PR	proportional representation
PR	relative portrayal
TI	Transparency International
UDHR	Universal Declaration of Human Rights
UNCAC	United Nations Convention against Corruption
VAW	violence against women
VSS	voting system standards

PREFACE

Politics plays a major role in the society, especially in the shaping up of a nation and consequently the world. It has been an integral part of the system and continues to be so even in the present times. The importance of politics assumes around the world can be catered to its role in determining the people who are responsible for forming the policies and laws and regulations which help in the forward development of a country and its progress.

Politics is characterized by power and money, owing to its obvious benefits as a politician is able to reach a huge audience and help them with their issues and problems. A politician generates a lot of respect for themselves as they try to resolve the issues being faced by needy people.

All these benefits make it the most lucrative role in a society and this also makes it the most vulnerable to crimes. Unfortunately, crime has been a major thorn in the political systems across the world and has been a hurdle in various political activities. It has got itself stuck to politics very strongly and is a major concern for many people who dream of a clean political system.

This book tries to educate the readers on the various criminal aspects of politics and the ways of dealing with the criminal activities. It informs the readers about the meaning of politics and the role played by crime in determining the political occurrences.

The readers are further informed about the big influence of money in politics, owing to the importance it holds in the current world. They are also told about the various kinds of voting systems and the way they affect the politics of a place. The chapters throw light on the role of judiciary in mitigating the crimes and ensuring justice and the impact it has in the judicial setup.

The book also makes the readers aware about the various human rights and how their violation takes place in a political setup. It talks about the way human rights are taken for granted by the politicians and what they must do to ensure those rights.

Corruption is also a major hurdle in the achievement of political goals. However, corruption is also a major form of crime that the people undertake to come in power. The book uncovers various forms of corruption and talks about the ways in which it can be curbed and fought.

The readers are further informed about the role of gender in politics and how the genders are treated differently in the political setup. It states the importance of proportional representation (PR) of the genders in the political setup. The book ends by talking about the ways in which politics can be decriminalized and a better environment can be created.

I hope that this book is sufficiently insightful on the various kinds of crimes that take place in politics and the way in which they impact various other things in a society.

Chapter 1

Crime and Politics: A Global Perspective

CONTENTS

Politics is a field that has been there for a long time and is believed to have existed from the very beginning of the human race. Politics is an essential part of a nation's system as well as it regulates various policies and determines the people who are good to take the responsibilities of the state in those regards.

However, as politics attains such significance in the society, the field becomes more and more criminalized. The lure of power gets the criminal activities involved with it. This chapter gives a global perspective over the relation of crime and politics all over the world.

1.1. INTRODUCTION

Criminal organizations play an important role in politics in many countries (even in rich ones. The main and common strategy of the gangdom groups in all countries is to use money and power to get their captured candidates elected in roles of public workers and procurement contractors.

This not only helps criminal organizations to get business opportunities and misusing public funds but also weakens the enforcement against the criminal organizations. Sometimes, such organizations use terror and violence to get their captured member elected.

In the politics arena, violence has been used for several purposes like honest candidates been terrorized so that the candidate who is less qualified or frightened or overawed gets elected in order to make them do what these criminal organizations want.

Honest candidates can be threatened by destroying their offices and harassing their campaign workers in order to cause disturbance or problems in their election campaign.

The criminal organizations use man force to threaten voters in order to vote against the honest candidates and get their candidate elected by capturing voting booths, etc. Lastly, the violence is used to threaten the elected honest politician so either he steps back or works under the influence of this criminal organization.

Sadly, politics and crime are related from the times of tribal leadership. Crime is said to be a political crime if it is committed to harm the state, government of the state, or political system. The crime would not be called political crime if any politician commits a crime against his family or wife or any crime committed by him due to his personal enmity.

For example, if the chief minister assaults his wife then this crime would be categories as domestic violence, not a political crime. However, if the same person uses his power to benefit the corporation by either bribing the lawyer or pressurizing the government authorities then it is a political crime.

The above example thus confirms that it is not necessary that all political crimes need to be violent, they can occur without the use of violence and terror too. In spite of not being crime categorization as a political crime in the United States, the individuals have been punished and prosecuted in the past.

The criminals keep in mind not to harm the country but despite of their good intentions, the accused is convicted with severity and harshness. Instead of labeling the crime under any header, these cases are handled individually.

1.2. WHAT IS POLITICS AND WHY IT IS IMPORTANT?

Politics can be defined as activities associated with the governance of a country area, especially the debate between the parties having power. All of us are somehow influenced by the term 'Politics' no matter how much we deny and claim not to be affected by it.

1.2.1. Defining Politics

Politics is the set of activities associated with the governance of the country, state, or area. It basically involves decision making, preservation, amendment of the rules under which people of that, particular area lives. It refers to achieving and exercising positions of governance-organized control over a human community, particularly as a state. Some people study these activities academically called political science (Figure 1.1).

Politics is intrinsically related to disputes, disagreements, and working together at the same time. On the one hand, the fact of having different needs, conflicting opinions, challenging differences of human races, and opposing interests assure disagreement of the rules and regulations which people follow.

However, on the other hand, people acknowledge the importance of working together in order to uphold the set rules. It draws upon Hannah Arendt's notion of 'acting in concert' in order to illustrate the ways that live hip hop shows be interactive spaces of collective identity and coordinated political practice.

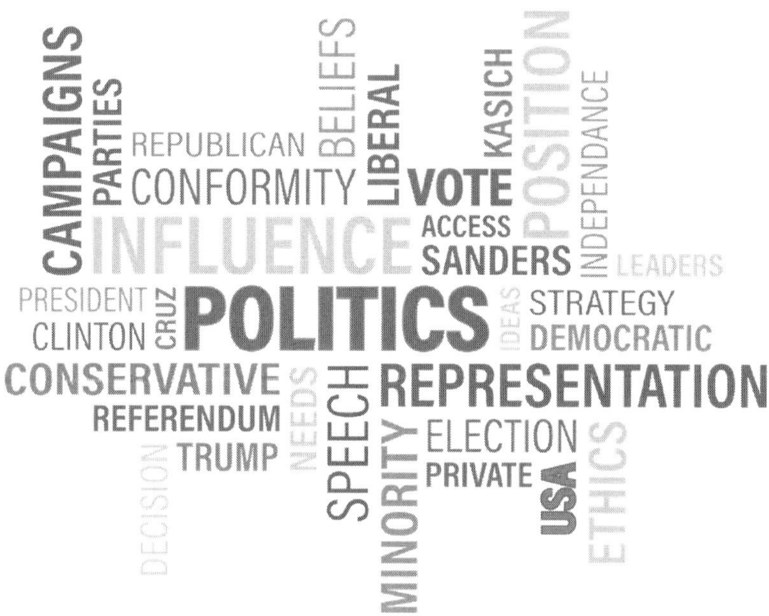

Figure 1.1: Politics is a huge part of the society and has been one of the oldest professions in the world.

Source: Image by Pixabay.

The heart and soul of the politics is the process by which two or more parties engaged in a disagreement, dispute or debate reach an agreement resolving it, in which people with different views and diverse polarities and mindset come together to live in the same country with same rules and regulations.

However, politics can be considered as a process or search of the peaceful ending of conflict and retribution than its attainment, as it is not possible to resolve all the conflicts and bring hindered percent harmony to the state. None the less, the inevitable existence of diversity (all are different) and dearth (insufficiency of resources) ensures that politics is an unavoidable aspect of human life.

The two major issues occur while defining the politics, the first one is politics is related to different areas and can be defined in very different way. 'Politics' is most is a term that influences audience by using appeal to emotion or stereotypes (Figure 1.2).

Figure 1.2: Politics determines the way in which the world will run.

Source: Image by Pikrepo.

Politics is not considered as an academic subject like economics, history, biology, etc. and it is so obviously assumed the teachers and students of political science are impartial and there are very few people who come to politics without any presupposition.

Worse is, people consider word politics as dirty as it has a bad image that always causes trouble, violence, devious influence, fraud. To the dismay of the time, there is nothing new in such kind of thought about politics. In the past in 1775, Johnson Samuel, an English writer quoted "Politics are now nothing than means of rising in the world.

With this sole view do men engage in politics and their whole conduct proceeds upon it." Henry Brooks Adams was an American historian, long back in the nineteenth century; he called politics as 'systematic organizations of hatred.' The hardest and second problem is that eve authorities concur with what the subject is about.

Politics, in its broadest sense, is the activity through which people make, preserve, and amend the general rules under which they live. It refers to achieving and exercising positions of governance – organized control over a human community, particularly as state.

1.3. POLITICS AS THE ART OF GOVERNMENT

As stated by Otto von Bismarck, aristocrat, and German statesman, "Politics is not a science, as the professors are apt to support. It is an art." The art Bismarck was quoting was art of governance, an art of controlling society with enforcement of laws and rules and by making collective decisions.

This was one of the classical definitions developed from the Ancient Greek meaning of politics, i.e., 'affairs of the cities,' and polis means "city-state.' Greece in the archaic period was made up from independent states, called Polis or city-state and every state has its own government.

Athens gave birth to democracy and other Greek states also established a similar politic system. Consequently, we can define 'politics as what concerns the poleis or the modern form is 'what affects the city or stated.' In this regard, it is clearly obvious that in the everyday use of the term: it is said "in politics" when people hold public office and 'entering politics" when they are planning to seek to do so.

The academic political science has also helped in conserving the definition of politics. In several ways, it is believed that it's just an idea and traditional belief that politics is "what concerns the state,' mainly noted in an academic study which focuses on the people and mechanism of the politics.

'The authoritative allocation of values,' these analytics came from David Easton, a Canadian-American political scientist of the 21st century. More precisely, it means politics is the system where one group or another gets to determine how society will operate and can compel adherence to their set of preferred values through laws, sanctions, and rewards.

Authoritative values are those which are accepted by few and are imposed on masses for the peaceful management of the state or country. The recent example is CAA acts in India which had cause several protests by a particular community in the country, however, it is accepted by few.

Therefore, we can easily say that politics is about policies and amendments in rules and laws with affirm decision making by the ruling government (governing body) to form a concrete and organized plan of action for the community. However, what is most noticeable about this definition is that it offers a highly confined perspective of politics.

Politics mean what is happening within a polity, i.e., an organized society, a state and political entity, the rules and regulations that are being formed in Legislations, government offices, cabinet rooms, etc. and decisions made by politicians, government servants, and lobbyists, etc., those who work within the machinery of government.

It clearly means that institutions which do not play any role in decision making or activities related with running of the country are non-political. In the same way, if we define politics as an activity which is only restricted to state-related or governing issues than we ignore the exponentially increasing global influences on today's so-called modern life, as we are going to discuss in our next section.

Though this definition can be restricted further, this is obvious in the proclivity to treat politics as the equivalent of party politics. In other words, the sphere of 'political' is limited to those state actors who are premeditatedly motivated by characteristics or set of a belief of a political party.

In this manner, politicians are called political, however, civil servants are called non-political, considering, and they are absolutely honest and professional in their job. Judges are considered non-political though they are related to law and they are the ones who make decisions of cases in law court, for example, judges were the ones who took the recent decision on demolition of Babri Masjid in India.

However, if their judgment is unfairly prejudiced due to some pressure of government or personal preferences (faith in a particular religion) then they would be indicted for being 'political.' A relation between the politics and the matters that government of the country deals with justifies the fact that why the politics is considered so derogatory and disparaging.

The reason behind it is that it is known popularly that politics is about the activities of the politician. However, the politician is those people who want to be in the power and become the part of the government themselves so that they can fulfill their personal ambitions by becoming a part of civil services (Figure 1.3).

Figure 1.3: There are many prominent entities involved in politics and governance of a state and its people.

Source: Image by Pixfuel.

They want to be part of the body that reflects the beliefs and interest of the nations and political system. The new generation is completely anti-politics as everyone has this common perception that politics is about corruption and dishonesty, the media has played an important role in forming this opinion.

The belittling phrases like "office politics" and "politicking" are associated by the image of politics as politics is viewed as self-serving, two-faced and unprincipled activity by the masses.

The writing of Niccolo Machiavelli also shows the same image of politics in his book "who is the Prince" in 1961. Then developed the image of political leaders as cunning, cruel, and manipulative and drew the attention of the people on the negative image of politics.

The widespread approach was developed by such a negative view of politics that people in power exploit their position for personal advantage at the expense of others as politicians are individuals who are corrupt and believe in self-service.

"Power tends to corrupt, and absolute power corrupts absolutely' is a famous saying by Lord Acton. Nonetheless, the unavoidable and continuing feature of politics for social existence is doubted by the people who view politics as corrupted power.

But corrupt politicians are always with our view no matter how reluctant they are to the fact that politics is a corrupted power.

As the early social contract theorists argued that without some kind of mechanism for allocation authoritative values, society would simply disintegrate into a civil war of all against each other. So, it is important to check and guarantee that governmental power is not abused by corrupt politicians, and politics is conducted within a framework rather than to abolish politicians and bring politics to end.

1.4. POLITICS AS PUBLIC AFFAIRS

The second broader inception of politics brings it beyond the limited sphere of government to what is called "public affairs" or public life. Or we can say that difference between political and non-political accord with the distinction between public sphere(is an area in a social life where individuals can come together to freely discuss and identify societal problems and through that discussion influence politics) of life and private sphere(a sector of societal life in which an individual enjoys a degree of authority, unhampered by interventions from government or other institutions; for example, home, and family.

And this view of politics reminds us of Aristotle, the famous Greek philosopher. In his politics, Aristotle believed that the man was a political animal because he is a social creature with the power of speech and moral reasoning.

According to him, human beings are able to live together by creating laws that enable both community survival and individual flourishing. Human possess the sense of both general and special justice thus they are the only one species that can create a just society, that is why Aristotle called politics as the master science on which all branches of human activity depends.

Politics is no less central to an understanding of our own society and the world around us. Public and private are contested realms; open to debate, and intervention. In one sense, the public may be addressed primarily as an issue of politics, as Jurgen Habermas (1991) and Hannah Arendt (1998) consider it in their work on the public sphere, debating who the public is and how the public expresses itself.

Public and private are social constructs that conceptualize different domains of everyday life-from the interiority and privacy of our bodies and homes to the publicness of city streets and public space. Issues of public and private transect class, racial, and gender lines and the forms of contestation vary from place to place.

And the above explanation of public and private realms observer the clear distinction between state and civil society. 'Social society is the entirety of all public and private relations and interactions among all the people of society' for example, all the government bodies lie to police, courts, army, etc. can be considered as public as they are responsible for cumulative structuring of society.

Also, their source of income is tax of common man, so it could be put as public servants working for public on their expenses only indirectly. Contrary to public, civil society comprises of what Edmund Burke called 'little platoons' – family, church, and local community-that orient men toward virtue such temperance and fortitude, according to him life begins there. Also, the groups that are working for themselves and run on their personal finances and interests are called 'private' as they are not working for larger society and for the interest of the public. Taking into account public and private division, politics is only limited to the activities and responsibilities of the state. The activities which are managed by individuals themselves like cultural, personal, domestic, etc. are called non-political.

Public and private can be further divided into finer distinctions called political and personal. Civil society means all the non-government, private, economic, social, cultural, moral recreational, and other such associations and institutions of the people.

Some political experts make a clear distinction between state and civil society. The state is organized single political community of all the people living in a territory who have organized government which makes laws (Legislative function performed by the Legislature) enforces the laws (Executive function performed by the Executive) and applies laws to specific cases (judicial functions performed by the judiciary).

The state is the sovereign community of all the people and its government is the coercive structure which makes and implements authoritative laws, rules, policies, decisions, and punishments. Against this, "Civil society works outside the state structure and belongs to the realm of autonomous associations and groups formed by individuals in their capacity as private citizens."

Civil society is worked by the people with the help of their own resources and efforts. All non-governmental private organizations, associations, and institutions including groups constitute the civil society. It refers to the non-political sonic-economic realm, distant from the state.

Though civil society is beautifully distinguished from state, in spite of that, there are many institutions like educational institutions and hospitals which are open for people. The critical inference of this is that it widens our conception of the political, particularly transferring of economy, from the private to public sphere. Even a workplace could be the playground of political players.

However, this view regarding organization such as clubs, trade unions, community groups, and businesses, it remains a confined view of politics. This outlook of political thinkers, the 'personal' affairs, and institution should not be infringed by politics.

Some women rightist is of opinion that politics has no place in the family and in domiciliary affairs; it has no existence in family life, home, and relationships. This perspective of feminists can be embellished by an example of a politician's ability to separate their personal and professional life completely.

By differentiating the two, say if he is cheating on his wife or doing any domestic violence and has not been good to his children, then it would be treated as his personal affair, and it can be denied to affect his political importance of his such act as it has nothing to do with his public affairs.

The outlook of politics as basically 'concerning the people as a whole' has given rise to both positive and negative images of politics. If we go back in the time of Aristotle, he is often seen as supporting the view that politics and political activity belong to the good life itself.

This argument was completely supported by Hannah Ardent, in her book 'The Human Condition' as she believed politics is an idea of active citizenship that is, on the value and importance of civic engagement and collective deliberation about all matters affecting the political community and argued that politics is the most important for human as it involves free discussion of equal citizens.

According to her 'each man is unique, so that with each birth something uniquely new comes into the world' (HC, 117–8). HC refers to her 'Human condition.'

Politics in this way brings meaning to life and assure each individual is unique. Theorists Jean Jacques Rousseau and John Stuart Mill who portrayed political participation as a good in itself have drawn the same conclusions.

Rousseau believed that people recognized 'their general will.' This general will is supposed to represent the common or public interest- and it is something that each individual has hand in making. According to him, all citizens should participate and should be committed to the general good even if it means eating against their private or personal interests.

For example, one should support a political party that proposes to tax us heavily because we can see the benefit that this taxation can bring to all. One of the central tenets of Mill's political outlook is that not only the rules of society, but also people themselves are capable of improvement and if they get involved in public affairs then they would be developed morally, personally, and ineffectually as public affairs are educational in nature.

Conversely, politics as a public activity has also been depicted as an undesired intervention. Particularly, liberal theorists prefer civil society over the state as they believe that the former gives more options and freedom to choose from different areas, and individuality is respected more in civil society. In this way, politics clearly prevent people from acting according to their choices and they want to keep it away from their family and private life and personal activities like business and sports.

1.5. POLITICS AS POWER

The third definition of Politics is comprehensive and is more absolute. This perspective sees politics in every sphere of human activities and social existence and does not restrict it to the only public realm. As indicated clearly in Adrian Leftwich's book 'what is Politics? Activity and its study (2004), "politics is at the heart of all collective social activity, formal, and informal, public, and private, in all human groups, institutions, and societies.'

From the above statement of Adrian, it is clear that politics takes place in each and every aspect of human activity, being it within the family member, workplaces. Politics do play an important role when it comes to interaction with neighboring countries or worldwide and thus, its existence is prominent at the level of any social interaction.

Extensively, the social survival depends on politics related to production, distribution, and usage of resources. In essentiality, Politics is power, its ability to achieve whatever it wants through any means. This conception was summarized by Harold Lassewell, in his book Politics:

Who gets what, when, How? He defined values as desired goals and power as ability to participate in decisions, and he conceived political power as the ability to produce intended effects on other people.

From this outlook, politics is about diversity and disagreement, but the necessary component is survival of dearth, no matter what the needs and desire of human cannot be limited and the resources present to fulfill those desires are never enough. Therefore, Politics could be called a struggle between high demand and short supply of resources and this struggle is conducted by the means of power (Figure 1.4).

Figure 1.4: The power and authority over the people and a state is also a major aspect of politics.

Source: Image by SVG Silh.

1.6. IMPORTANCE OF POLITICS

Politics is more in the picture when elections are near; however, in a country like India, politic is always the topic of conversation among common people and some or other kind of elections is always coming up here.

Although, some people do not have any clue what Politics is about but still everyone has their own opinions and judgment about political activities happening around them. The question arises is their opinion valid? Are we fully aware of Political activities going on in our country or in the work?

Politics play an important role, and similar elections play an important role too. Political activities are not only taking place during elections but also in our daily lives. And our daily life is not only affected by Democratic and Republican politics but by every law and governmental rule.

Everything, our schools, our municipality, town, city, states, country get affected by Politics. It's the misconception of the people that if it seems nothing is happening right away then it means that politics is not doing anything, however, it is not the reality, and actually, things are happening at the backend. As a nation, we fail to understand the real essence of political activities happening all the time and it's dreadful. And it is more dreadful to think that your opinion doesn't matter and you should stop voicing your concerns.

Our present conditions and life are what because of the decisions taken by the political parties in the past and in the present regarding our rights and welfare at the state and country level. None of us tunes in to listen to the parliamentary meetings held every day that decide the things that will affect us directly.

People would complain about high taxes they are paying but no one tries to figure out where that high amount of money which has been deducted in the form of tax from their hard-earned money is used. Politicians are easily escaping by telling lies and stealing as no one pays much attention to the details or pinpoint them legally.

If one is not satisfied with the work of the current elected legislative of their locality or city or state or country, one has the power to throw them out of their elected seat. Our main problem is that we are not aware of many of our rights and duties towards nation and we underestimate the power of the citizen of a country.

The country is formed by we the people not we the government and government are formed by 'we, the people' to serve the country, if each one of us use our rights properly then we can make our country the way we want it.

1.6.1. The Politics of Crime

The crime has been the major problem of the world in the past decade; it's been a persistent matter of concern for the people. When surveys are conducted across the world to find out the major concerns of the people and their opinion then Crime is at the top of the list.

However, when it comes to electing a candidate, they put their priority of finding a person who could eradicate crime and other concerns take front seat. And the excuse they provide for such Behavior is that no one can do much about the problem of rising crime in the country.

This attitude of people is misguided as something can be done about the crime. Though, it is correct that this fact can be proven with scientific precisions, however, some of the criminal facts are clear.

Due to presence of officers on streets and subways, alert family members, neighborhood, the crimes in the few big cities is controlled. However, in courtrooms, many of the accused do not get the punishment as per the crime is committed. For example, if a person is convicted of robbery and deserves the imprisonment for 10 years is granted plea and his punishment duration reduces to 3 years.

The reason behind it is that system cannot afford to have more criminals. The prisons are overcrowded, judges are exhausted, each, and everyone in the criminal courts including the police.

Many people are against this process of working by a criminal court because according to them, plea bargaining returns criminals on the street and the crime rate is increasing day by day in the United States. However, few of the people contemplated the figure shown by surveys conducted in New York, In New York; every year arrests 104,000 burglars, robbers, arsons, etc.

However, it has capacity of five thousand jury trials per year. Therefore, New York authorities been forced to do the same as other states official are following, dropping charges or reducing their term of sentence through plea bargaining. It requires a lot of money for police, prosecutors, judges, and jails to put all the criminals in jail to decrease the crime rate as many criminals are free.

The biggest question arises is that why steps have not been taken to reduce the crime when it can be done and more surprising is that answers are complicated and each step gets opposed by some organized powerful groups. This uncooperative group often includes middle-class interests those who have always complained about the threat of crime very frequently.

It is believed that the problem is associated with American courts. And the American courts here mean judges, attendants, judicial staffs or clerks and secretaries, this definition is considered by laypeople, however, actually 'courts' must include all the supporting agencies that either supply power to criminals to the judges or receive them after judgment.

When the 'courts' are interpreted in this way then people would be able to estimate the actual cost of improving these operations. The cost of increasing the policemen and prosecuted would be so high that people would have to pay very high taxes and this cost would be much higher than the cost people are paying as victims of crime.

It is often the case that people who are mostly the victims of the crimes happening in the States are the people who know nothing about how public money is spend and pay very low taxes and live in ghettos (places where people of a minority group live) or have neighborhoods which are not safe and include people with very low income and they themselves also work at places like gas stations or all night diners which are easy spots of crime.

And the taxpayers who would be paying the double tax to improve the criminal court lives in the safe and protected neighborhood and send their children to private and protected schools. Also, they can afford private security forces in order to protect their houses.

Though, the middle class of the United States might not be in favor of paying the increased cost for enforcement to reduce the crime rate. However, the incurred cost of enforcement would be less that the cost of crime in the country run at present; it costs a hundred of billions of dollars every year to the country.

For example, 3 to 7% of all merchandise which is displayed in the showrooms or shops account for shoplifting and that cost is included the price of customer's purchase, so eventually, the buyer has to pay 3 to 7% up the normal price which would be summed up much more than the increased taxes they have to pay for increased enforcement to curb the crime rate in the United States (Figure 1.5).

Figure 1.5: Crime is a bitter truth of the political scenarios around the globe.

Source: Image by Pixabay.

Besides, revenue is even generated by criminal courts and its supporting agencies, for example, the traffic department and lower courts generate more revenue through fines and fees they charge from the defaulter than the actual cost needed to run them.

The treasury is filled with fines when local and state business regulations are enforced. Also, the property, industry, commerce business would increase if the crime rate would decrease. This would also increase the values of property and a stronger tax base.

Also, it's not only to do with budget constraints in the case of lack of funds for the courts, however, it could be the probability that it is done deliberately and purposefully and it has nothing to do with the budget.

1.6.2. People's View of Crime Depends on the Politics

The study in the British Journal of Criminology shows that even decades later, the perception of crime of people is influenced by different political periods in which they 'came of age.'

Researchers are trying to find out the origin and inferences of people's fear of crime for forty years. However, to date, no such facts have been put forward which clearly shows that if there is any relation or effect on a group of people who grew up in a particular political period on their emotional responses to crime.

People are more sensitive to social events and also form key opinions during the age of 15–25, when they are growing up and cohort would have the same opinion about crime and politics what they have experienced at that age.

Researchers from the University of Sheffield, University of Southampton and Sciences Po, Paris, surveyed and tried to examine methodically and in detail the data on fear of crime and unsocial Behavior from the British Crime Survey in England and Wales spanning 30 years.

Through this survey, they were able to guess the approximate of the net result of individual aging, the historical period in which the survey was conducted and political generation participants belonged too.

According to Researchers, there is strong relation between a participant's fear related to crime and their political generation. For example, there is the greatest level of fear housebreaking theft in the respondents who grew up the political period of Margaret Thatcher or John Major. It is the same generation which during 1980's has observed dramatic rise in property crime. At the same time, people of Wilson/Callagan generation had the highest level of concern for the theft and knockdown and this was the main cause of worry of journalists, politicians, and policymakers of the time.

The similar inference has taken out from the responses of anti-socialist behaviors. The highest level or worry was shown by people of age of Blair and Brown about problems like actions like deliberate destruction or damage to public or private property, teenage loaf, and noisy neighbors, such issues were highly highlighted by the people who concerned about making law at those times.

Majorly, this study emphasizes and cleared the fact that the people have a great natural tendency of fear the crimes that were the matter of concern of the politicians, lawmaker, journalist at the times of their youth and has affected their surroundings during the times of their adulthood.

The finding of the research clearly shows that crime fears can loiter and the attitude about crime can be influenced for long term by the process by which people from their political values.

Stephen Farrall, in one of the papers said, "The pronouncements leading politicians make about crime can have a lasting impact on the crime fears of young adults.

Political and popular debates about crime that are prevalent in one's youth appear to impact the fears those individuals report through adulthood and into middle age," The stories we hear about crime and suffering impact of our political history on us are affected by our narratives of crime and disorder.

1.7. ORGANIZED CRIME, VIOLENCE, AND POLITICS

In most of the countries, the political parties are captured by the criminal organizations. Then easily the allocation of public investment can be easily distorted by the captured politician toward the area of influence of criminal organization and encourage clemency act in their service.

There are many big questions like how the political parties are taken over by the criminal groups? How do the voting system, the potency of political competition and authorities of the institution get influenced by the game plan of criminal organizations?

The power of criminal organization can be measured by the violent crime committed by them and their capacity & inclination toward violence. This power of criminal organization not only impacts the Behavior of elected candidates but also creates panic in the members of non-captured political group and its workers.

First, the extent of pre-electoral violence is identified under various electoral rules and the degree of electoral competition. A necessary element of electoral campaigns in mass democracies is money to fund candidate or party campaigns (Figure 1.6).

Figure 1.6: Crime in politics also involves use of arms and hence loss of lives.

Source: Image by Needpix.

The electoral campaign financing model strategies (e.g., Persson and Tabellini, 1999; Lixxeri and Persico, 2001), under a region, promotional rule, the incentives to use violence depend on the comparable power of the truthful and dishonest political party at the national level of electoral competition, due to majoritarianism (it is a traditional political philosophy that a majority of the population has the right to make decisions that affect the society), violence is present in a high proportion in marginal districts relative to other districts as there is head to head completion between two parties.

This directive also helps to find out that where more money should be invested to win elections. For example, Akhmedov, and Zurahvaskya (2004), Brender, and Drazen (2005). Alt and Lassen (2006) provide evidence on this phenomenon: see Alsenia and Paradesi (2017) on the specific case of Italy.

Evidently, pyromania, violent acts which are not lethal, killing, murder, interruption in campaign activities, etc. are initiated to affect the voting system. The more focus is on homicide as more data is available on such events and are reported openly as there is no way to hide them.

Though, the number of homicides in a region is the best way to measure organized crime violence. This data is available for almost all Italians since 1887 and this is advantageous for us. In a region with a significant presence of organized crime, the significant increase in homicides at the times of election, and it is the findings of the results of the research on Silicon Mafia victims.

Comparison of the extent of pre-electoral violence under different institutional regimes, electoral systems, and level of electoral competition is possible due historical coverage of these data by us. The interesting fact is that, criminal organization was present in all time and was associated with high pre-electoral violence except during the fascist dictatorship (1922–1943).

The criminal organizations had no influence during the times of Hitler and Benito as it is the form of government that is a type of one-party dictatorship. However, in democracy, there is huge scope of electoral violence due to degree of electoral competition and big difference of rules of elections.

Predictive modeling helped us to find that pre-electoral violence increased with increasing electoral competition at the national level under cumulative voting; under the majoritarian system, pre-electoral violence is concentrated in marginal districts.

1.8. THE INDESTRUCTIBLE CRIME-TYPE

The oldest of all crime types is the political crime. The political crimes have been recorded in every society and it is impossible to find any society which has not witness political crimes. The political criminals have been present in the society in the past, present, and will be present in the future.

The tragedy is that design behind the plot of political crime is often destroyed as soon as it is executed and become real despite of its historical nature. Criminologist has completely ignored the political crime though it occurs again repeatedly and is the eldest type of crime.

It has become the body which is just spying the crimes and often termed as 'Criminological satellite,' a strange body law infringement revolving around the concept of crimes of ordinary nature. The most surprising is how criminologist can fail to analyze the data on political crime though it is available extensively and it seems there is no hurdle in studying the facts.

The most profound political changes can be viewed in the modern twentieth-century history. All the changes during that period for example, rise, and fall of empires, races, classes, social systems, and charismatic involved political crimes.

The unduly observable attitude of modern criminology is may be more interested in Behavior and results of conduct than comportment itself. Moreover, it should be facilitated by criminologist that most of the criminal have common behaviors and characteristics especially political criminals.

Political criminals steal style from one another and are often termed as methodological kleptomaniacs. Even the writers have acknowledged the political criminal in the past as intense felon; the political criminals are high tech modern criminals though they look old-styled people.

The feeling of worry is more obvious with increasing number of revolutions, social protests, and disruptions as the problem of political crime are becoming more contemporary. So far, this worry is not raised from resistance to a better future, but from the confusion jeopardized by varicolored and antimetrical proposals for the new political model.

From a period of time, human societies have often been shaped by political crimes; we are living in an era in which the bad effects of political criminality are so easily available for us than its uses.

Gustave Le Bon was leading French polymath, who claimed several characteristics of crowd philosophy in his book in 1895, according to him "an individual immersed for some length of time in a crowd soon finds himself-either in consequence of magnetic influence given out by the crowd or from some other causes of which we are ignorant-in a special state, which much resembles the state of fascination in which the hypnotized individual finds himself in the hands of the hypnotizer.

His vision proves to be 100% correct in the twentieth century or we can say in the eighteenth century, he correctly predicted the future. Tragically, the term 'restructuring' has lost its real meaning and instead truly structuring the system, the term has become mixed up ideas of revolutionary alterations in society.

fail to understand the social and consider the man as guilty. For example, Bhagat Singh was hanged to death by the British government, however, he was a great reformist and now after centuries, his image has raised to Saint. Austin's particular theory of law is often called the 'command theory of law,' which states that the law is the command of the sovereign, backed by the threat of sanction in the event of non-compliance,' assuming that all the laws that are formulated represent the right value system, even though all the members of the society do not believe so.

The ruling social power is responsible to define the law as long as it prevails in power and they would be considered 'just' as long as they exist in the power, this fact should be understood by all the people who are ambitious to become political criminals. It is the social power, not political criminals who decided what is right and wrong.

The wonderful story of captured Pirate was told by Cicero where pirate defended in front of Alexander, the great that he is been considered pirate instead of great warrior simply because his boat is smaller than Alexander's large armada as he was doing the same thing as Alexander is doing. And the point raised by the pirate was simple.

The question of who has the power had right to declare what is 'right' and 'wrong' is an old problem and has been a topic of study for jurists as well as sociologist. And this problem is continuing for long because lawyers are too close and sociologist are too far and both are unwilling and hesitant to meet in the realm of sociology of law, which is also called legal philosophy.

It takes so much to create a law, usually, people with different values come together to form and they have to agree at one point.

Still, in the end, use of Herbert Hart's term, "a penal statue declaring certain conduct criminal' may appear to be the gunman situation writ large. John Austin believed that the law is the command of the royalty and may well be a terrifying truth which offers little shelter for those who abandon the real world for the comfort of illusions.

The largest barrier in understanding this belief is our disinclination to accept the fact that it is not necessary that whatever we think is right is the only right view. We incline to think that there is a single unchangeable truth, and arrive at the judgment that there is only one possible system of justice.

The doubtful theory that there is one normal and ethical code claims that the social system and its law are moral or ethical. The beliefs of the people who are involved in political crime that their right and values are just permit them to break the law. However, the brutal reality is that value system can only be defined by social-political power. It has the right to define 'right' and 'wrong' of the system of human Behavior. And these set of values defined by social power by those who are involved with the social system for the time that social power exists. The mindset or the philosophy of the political criminals depends on the mindset of the prevailing social power.

1.10. CONCLUSION

Crime and politics have been interrelated from the time of tribal. While politics holds great importance in the context of a nation or a state, the crime involved in it makes it a field that is not safe to take up as a profession or responsibility.

There are various kinds of crimes involved in politics ranging from corruption, money laundering, mass killings, theft, and discriminatory practices to denying human rights or civil rights to the people. The study of criminology helps in identifying the various aspects of politics which are exposed to crime and help to rectify them so that they do not impact the lives of other people.

Politics must be capable of providing the people with the proper governance and necessities so that they can lead their lives in an independent way and in a manner, they want it to be. It must be made free of crime and must be for the people.

REFERENCES

1. Alesina, A., Piccolo, S., & Pinotti, P., (2016). *Organized Crime, Violence, and Politics*. [eBook] Available at: http://scholar.harvard.edu/files/alesina/files/organized_crime_violence_politics_march_2016.pdf?m=1456945412 (accessed on 25 April 2020).
2. Alesina, A., Piccolo, S., & Pinotti, P., (2018). Organized crime, violence, and politics. *The Review of Economic Studies*, [online] *86*(2), pp. 457–499. Available at: https://academic.oup.com/restud/article/86/2/457/5060718 (accessed on 25 April 2020).
3. EurekAlert!. (2018). *How People View Crime Depends on the Politics of When They Were Growing Up*. [online] Available at: https://www.eurekalert.org/pub_releases/2018–08/oupu-hpv080618.php (accessed on 25 April 2020).
4. Madison, E., (n.d.). *Politics and Crime*. [online] Study.com. Available at: https://study.com/academy/lesson/political-crime-definition-lesson.html (accessed on 25 April 2020).
5. Matysek, K., (2016). *The Importance of Politics*. [online] The Odyssey Online. Available at: https://www.theodysseyonline.com/the-importance-of-politics (accessed on 25 April 2020).
6. n.d. *What Is Politics?* [eBook] Available at: https://www.macmillanihe.com/resources/sample-chapters/9780230363373_sample.pdf (accessed on 25 April 2020).
7. Neely, R., (1982). *The Politics of Crime-82.08*. [online] Theatlantic.com. Available at: https://www.theatlantic.com/past/docs/politics/crime/neelycri.htm (accessed on 25 April 2020).
8. Schafer, S., (1972). The concept of the political criminal. *Journal of Criminal Law and Criminology*, [online] *62*(3). Available at: https://scholarlycommons.law.northwestern.edu/cgi/viewcontent.cgi?article=5732&context=jclc (accessed on 25 April 2020).
9. UpJourney-Live a Happy, Healthy and Successful Life, (2019). *What is Politics and Why is it Important? (According to 4 Experts)*. [online] Available at: https://upjourney.com/what-is-politics-and-why-is-it-important (accessed on 25 April 2020).

Chapter 2

Money and Politics

CONTENTS

Money and politics highlight the big role that money plays at the time of the electoral process and how the money supply corrupts the economy. Initially, this article talks about the how money plays a crucial role in campaign financing which not only helps the candidates or political parties but also creates awareness among voters towards building an inclusive democracy.

A remarkable knowledge about three different functions of money in the form of medium of exchange, store of value, and unit of account. Further, this article takes a brief look at the perspective of some economists who gave several approaches to explain the concept of money.

The article also talks about the involvement of money in economy stand in the way of for the middle class. Over the last generation, the middle class has faced stagnating opportunities for advancement, increasing health and education costs, and weakened job and retirement security.

Despite this, the government has too often failed to respond, or their way of response has made the problem worse. Somehow, money has inserted itself to the core of the country's progress. In the later stages, the article talks about the most important and still prevailing problem in our society that is the involvement of money and media in politics.

The voter's appeal is lost due to the conniving and the elevated value placed in high-proficiency media, slick interest groups that use propaganda to persuade voter turn-out in electoral networks. In the end, we will get to know how reforming the laws is the only way that would assure that political parties cannot get the upper hand through money or media's influence during elections.

2.1. INTRODUCTION

Campaign financing, a widely debated term, is among the many factors crucial for the proper functioning of democracy. For some, money is a highly overrated term in politics that serves as an expression of an effective instrument and free speech.

It helps in creating awareness for voters and building an inclusive democracy. For others, if the money is used in unrestrained ways, it can disintegrate the proper functioning of democracy. As a result, it can lead to unequal access to power, excessive campaigning, and politicians who are beholden to special interest groups. In practice, the majority of the countries with political pluralism have adopted some kind of political finance regulation. One way or the other the ranging from information and disclosure requirements limits the campaign contributions or expenditures (Scarrow, 2007).

In countries like the UK and Canada, the parties and individuals have been following the same pattern for decades to limit the campaign. More recently, countries like Israel, France, New Zealand, Chile, South Korea, Belgium, and many others have also adopted campaign spending caps.

Further, giving a handful of contributions at limiting the role of money during elections. Despite the widespread adoption of spending money in limits, their influence on the political process has been challenging to quantify.

Theoretically, it affects the performance of both incumbent politicians and challengers while following the campaign spending limits. However, their effects depend on certain factors, whether incumbents have a higher voter disposition, whether their fund-raising efficiency is different or whether they have different campaign spending effectiveness (Che and Gale, 1998; Pastine and Pastine, 2012).

Most of the existing models acknowledge the case of two candidates. Many political environments display an incumbent that might compete against multiple challenges and the number of challenges that decide to run for an election depend on their expectations of campaign financing and spending.

Sometimes it becomes challenging to test the effects of spending the limits empirically because campaign finance reform is usually applied uniformly across elections and jurisdictions, making it difficult to identify an appropriate comparison group.

Moreover, spending caps might potentially affect not only the identity of who is elected but also who chooses to run. Few countries can provide information on their non-elected candidates, their characteristics, and their campaign spending patterns, which one way or the other renders an analysis of the effects of spending caps woefully incomplete (Figure 2.1).

The research, however, can contribute directly to a large literature that examines the aftereffects of how much spent during regulating campaigns (Austen-Smith, 1987; Coate, 2004; Ashworth, 2006; Prat, 2002).

According to a rich theoretical literature, that studies the effects of limits on campaign donations and spending (Che and Gale, 1998; Fang, 2002; Pastine and Pastine, 2012; Cotton, 2012), empirical studies are rare.

Figure 2.1: Money is crucial in all fields including politics.

Source: Image by Wallpaper Flare.

The potential endogeneity of spending caps is perceived as a key challenge to casual identification. It is indeed a fact that many nations around the world have implemented spending limits. However, their presence and magnitude are likely to be associated with other unobserved factors that also affect the potential outcomes.

According to Stratmann and Aparicio-Castillo's (2006) study, the effects of the introduction of contribution limits at the state level in the U.S. They discover the evidence that narrows the chances of winning candidates' margin of victory and increase the number of candidates.

To our understanding, Milligan and Rekkas (2008) is the only other empirical investigation of the effects of campaign spending limits. It studies the spending caps in Canadian federal elections.

Apart from the fact that limits are set by a formula which is a function of the number and the density of electors within each federal district, however, the authors find that higher limits are associated with higher incumbent spending, fewer candidates, and lower voter turnout.

Unions are important financial powerhouses in elections, but much of their spending is done in such a way that it doesn't show up on FEC reports—it involves getting out the vote or internal communication with their members rather than paid TV ads. And it often focuses on state and local races rather than federal ones. The Wall Street Journal's Tom McGinty and Brody Mullins analyzed union disclosures of political spending to the Labor Department and came up with these totals, which were much higher than previously known. In the 2010 election season, the AFL-CIO and its affiliated unions spent $608 million, the SEIU spent $150 million, and AFSCME (representing state, county, and municipal employees) spent $133 million. The vast majority of this money was spent in favor of Democratic candidates.

2.2. WHAT IS MONEY?

Money is any verifiable economic unit that is generally accepted as payment in exchange for goods and services, repayment of debts such as taxes, or any other transactional purposes in an economy. Money creates a platform for reducing transaction costs, namely the double coincidence of wants.

Figure 2.2: Money is a major player in the crime activities taking place around the globe.

Source: Image by Wallpaper Flare.

Money is a phenomenon of establishing a commodity, having a physical property to be facilitated by market participants as a medium of exchange. Money can be: market-determined, officially declared by the government to be legal tender or fiat money, electronic cryptocurrencies, and money substitutes, and fiduciary media (Figure 2.2).

2.3. UNDERSTANDING MONEY

Money in a most specific sense referred to as currency. Economically, each government has adopted some kind of money system. Cryptocurrencies are a form of digital currency that came into existence for financing and international exchange across the world.

Money is considered as a liquid asset that enables settlement of transactions. Its functions are determined through the general acceptance of its value within a governmental economy and internationally through foreign exchange.

With that being said, it is not necessarily what the current value of the monetary currency is derived from the materials used to produce the note or coin. Rather, Value is derived from the willingness and purpose for a displayed value and rely on its consumption in future transactions.

The primary function of money is generally acknowledged as a medium of exchange that people and global economies intend to hold as an intermediate money as a payment for current or future transactions.

The economic money system began a widespread sensation for the functioning of exchange. The use of money as currency for the transactional process creates a centralized medium for buying and selling in a market.

The purpose of money was not only for the exchange process but most importantly, it replaced the barter system. Monetary currency helps to create a platform that avoids the double coincidence of wants.

The double coincidence of wants is a long-standing universal problem in a barter economy, at the time of the trade, two parties each hold an item the other wants, and so they exchange these items directly without any monetary medium.

To be most valuable as money, a currency should be:

- Portable;
- Stable;
- Fungible;
- Durable; and
- Recognizable.

These attributes ensure that the advantage of eliminating or reducing the transaction cost of the double coincidence of wants is not burdened by other types of transaction costs associated with that specific good (Figure 2.3).

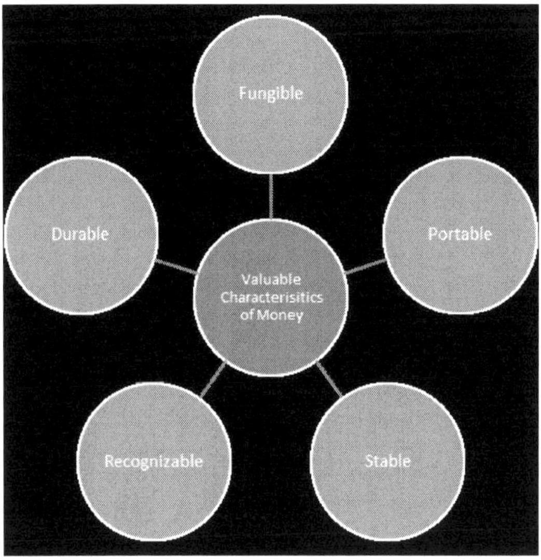

Figure 2.3: Characteristics of money to become valuable.

2.3.1. Fungible

Units of the good or a commodity should be of relatively uniform quality so that they are essentially interchangeable, and each of its parts is indistinguishable from another part.

The value for use in future transactions may not be consistent or reliable if different units of the good have different qualities. In case of using a non-fungible good as money may lead to transaction costs of individually evaluating each unit of the good before an exchange can take place.

2.3.2. Durable

The physical character of a commodity or a good should be durable enough to retain its value in future exchanges and can be used on multiple occasions. A perishable good or a good that degrades quickly with use in exchanges will not be beneficial for future transactions. In case of using non-durable goods as money conflicts with money's essentially future-oriented use-value.

2.3.3. Portable

Money should be portable and divisible into small denominations so that people appreciate its original use value highly enough. It would be worth the quantity of the good so that can be conveniently carried. A good of low original use-value, an indivisible good, and immovable good can create problems.

In case of using a non-portable good as money can produce transaction costs of either physically transporting large quantities of the low value good or defining practical, immobile object or transferable ownership of an indivisible.

2.3.4. Recognizable

The authenticity and quantity of the good should be easily ascertainable to the users so that they can easily be convinced of the terms of an exchange. In case of using a non-recognizable good as money can produce transaction costs of agreement on the authenticity and quantity of the goods by all parties to an exchange.

2.3.5. Stable

It is the value that people set on a good in exchange for other goods so that their willingness to trade should increase from time to time or stay relatively constant. A commodity consistently loses value over time or whose value varies widely up and down over time is less suitable.

In case of using a non-stable good as money produces transaction costs of repeatedly revaluing the good in each successive transaction. It also increases the risk of the exchange value of the good might drop below its other direct use-value or not be useful at all, in which case it will no longer circulate as money.

2.4. FUNCTIONS OF MONEY

There are three different functions of money. The static function of money serves as a medium of exchange, store of value, and unit of account.

A Medium of exchange is considered as one of the most significant factors of money that act to facilitate transactions. Without the flow of money, the barter system would be conducted for all types of transactions. Barter involves transactions directly exchange goods or services for other goods or services. However, the barter system has a huge drawback, while purchasing a particular good or service from a supplier; one has to possess an equivalent estimate of good or service, which the supplier also desires. In other words, a barter system can only take place if there is a double coincidence of wants between two or more transacting parties.

The possibility of a double coincidence of wants, however, is small and it makes the exchange of goods and services rather tough to take place. Money serves as a medium of exchange that is accepted in all transactions, by all parties, regardless of whether they desire each other's goods and services, and it effectively eliminates double coincidence of wants.

Store of value serves as that medium of exchange, where money must hold its value over time, that is, it must be a store of value. In other words, you can store the purchasing power of money and keep a part of it for future use, i.e., monetary savings.

However, if money could not be stored for a while and remain valuable in exchange, the problem of the double coincidence of wants will continue to persist and therefore, would not be utilized as a medium of exchange.

As a store of value, money is not freakish. Many other stores of value exist, such as stamps, works of art, even baseball cards and land. Money may not be considered as the best store of value because it deteriorates with inflation. However, money is said to be more liquid than most of the other stores of value because the purpose of serving as a medium of exchange is fulfilled as it is readily accepted everywhere. Furthermore, money is an easily transported store of value that is accessible in several convenient denominations. The unit of account is also one of the key functions of money. It functions as a unit of account, providing a *common standard for measuring relative worth* of goods and services being exchanged. Knowing the worth of price for goods and services. It enables both the purchaser and supplier of the good to make choices about how much of the good to purchase and how much of the good to supply.

2.5. THE DIFFERENT TYPES OF MONEY IN AN ECONOMY

2.5.1. Commodity Money

Commodity money has been used for thousands of years. Commodity money is a commodity that has value even if it is not being used as money. (It is usually stated as *intrinsic* value.) At the time of economic turmoil, it is believed that people sometimes prefer to commodity money rather than the money authorized by their governments.

Gold is believed to be a perfect example of commodity money considering they assert that gold has intrinsic value apart from its monetary properties. While it is worth noting that gold does have some uses. In most cities, gold is used for making jewelry and money rather than for making non-ornamental items.

2.5.2. Commodity-Backed Money

Commodity-backed money has a slight variation from commodity money. While commodity money is money whose commodity value comes from a *commodity* itself as currency directly, and commodity-backed money is backed with a commodity.

In other words, money can be traded in with a request. The gold standard is considered as the best example of the use of commodity-backed money. In the gold standard, people do not carry around gold as cash instead of trading gold directly for goods and services. However, the system worked in such a way that the currency holders could trade for a specified amount of gold in their currency.

2.5.3. Fiat Money

Fiat money is money with no intrinsic value. However, it has value as money because the government announced that it has value for that purpose. Even after being proclaimed as legal tender, the country need not hold its worth in commodity.

While somewhat counterintuitive, a monetary system using fiat money is surely possible and it is. In fact, most of the countries use it. Fiat money is feasible only because of these three key functions of moneya unit of account, a store of value, and a medium of exchange. These functions are destined to be fulfilled as long as all the people in a society recognize that the fiat money is a valid form of currency (Figure 2.4).

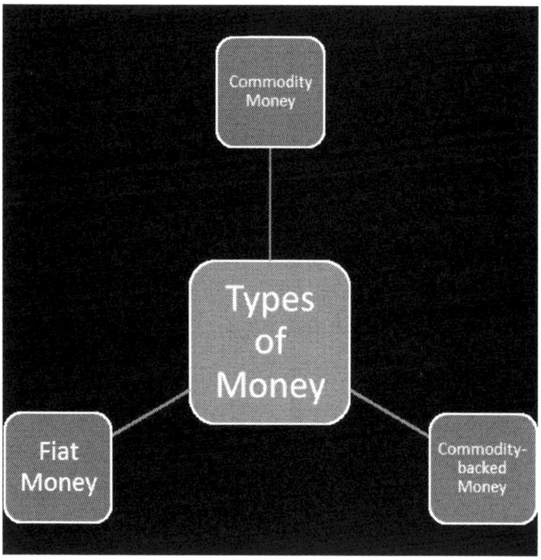

Figure 2.4: Different types of money.

2.5.4. Commodity-Backed Money vs. Fiat Money

It is the most widely debated political discussion that centers on the issue of the commodity (or, more precisely, commodity-backed) money versus fiat money. However, it may not be the case, in reality, the difference between the two isn't quite as large as people used to think.

This is because for two reasons. First, the major problem for fiat money is the absence of intrinsic value. With that being said, opponents of fiat money consider that a system using fiat money is inherently fragile because fiat money doesn't have a non-money value.

Considering this as a genuine concern, one must sincerely wonder how monetary system backed by gold is significantly different. With that being said, only a small fraction of the world's gold supply is used for making non-ornamental properties. Sometimes it looks like that, the gold is considered worth mostly because people believe it has value, much like fiat money?

Second, the competitors of fiat money claim that the unlimited ability of the government to print money whenever they want and without having to back it up with a specific commodity has a potential threat. This is also a valid concern up to some extent.

However, that is not entirely prevented by a commodity-backed money system, since it is almost certain for the government to harvest more of the

Yet, both these specifications are not strong enough to include time deposits in the definition of money.

- **Gurley-Shaw Approach:** According to this approach, the liabilities of non-banking financial intermediaries in the definition of money. The genius behind this approach was John G. Gurley and Edward S. Shaw. While explaining the concept of money, Gurley and Shaw emphasized the fact that the substitution relationship works among various factors, such as time deposits, currency, saving bank deposits, and demand deposits.

These factors serve as sources for storing value. Therefore, according to Gurley-Shaw, money can be defined as the weighted sum of demand deposits and several other types of deposits and currency. The claims against all the types of financial intermediaries. The weights should be granted based on the substitutability of currency.

However, such an implication of this approach is unlikely to take place as it is challenging to determine the degree of substitutability of deposits and claims against the financial intermediaries. Moreover, assigning weights to measure the money supply is a challenging task.

- **Central Bank Approach:** This approach has garnered favoritism from central banking authorities. It creates a broader view of the whole concept of money. The two key functions of the central bank are to control and regulate the flow of money in an economy. That is why the central bank facilitates the implementation of monetary policy to achieve its objectives and goals.

For this very purpose, the tasks proceed to all the sources and modes of payment and flow of credit in the economy, which are treated as money. Central bank view has stated that the currency and all other assets that can be turned into money (realizable assets) are included in the money supply.

It was the Radcliffe Committee of the United States that endorsed the central bank approach. According to this committee, "there is a similarity that persists between the currency and other realizable assets or means of purchasing to the point of rejecting money in favor of some broader concept, measurable or immeasurable."

In other words, money could be any form that gives credit to borrowers either through investment or commodity. Based on monetary policy and policy targets, the central bank executes different measures to regulate the money supply (Figure 2.6).

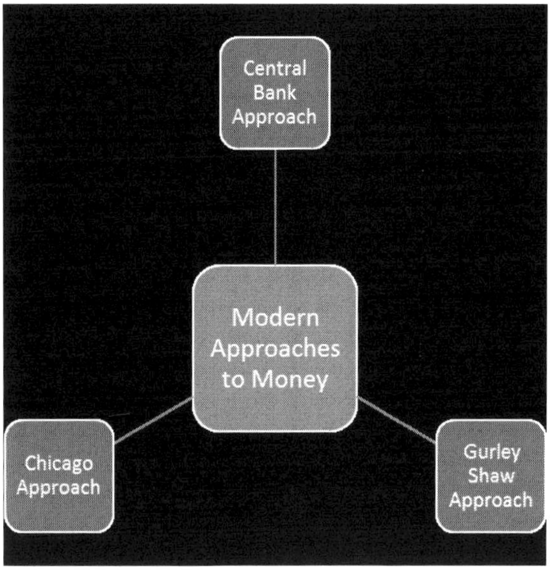

Figure 2.6: Modern approaches to money.

2.7. DEMAND FOR MONEY

The demand for money is slightly different from the demand for a commodity. On one hand, demand for money implies how many financial assets an individual or businessman wishes to hold, On the other hand, demand for a commodity implies the demand for the quantity or the continuous flow of goods and services that customers are willing to buy at a certain market price.

Therefore, a slight difference can be analyzed between the demand for money and demand for a commodity, where the former centers around holding, while later focuses on the flow. Initially, the demand for money was defined as the amount of money required for making business transactions.

In other words, the demand for money was highly dependent on the number of transactions made in an economy. As a consequence, there was a quick demand for money in the boom period, whereas at the time of depression the demand for money fell. Keynes stated a modern perspective on demand for money, i.e., demand for money is the demand for money to hold (Figure 2.7).

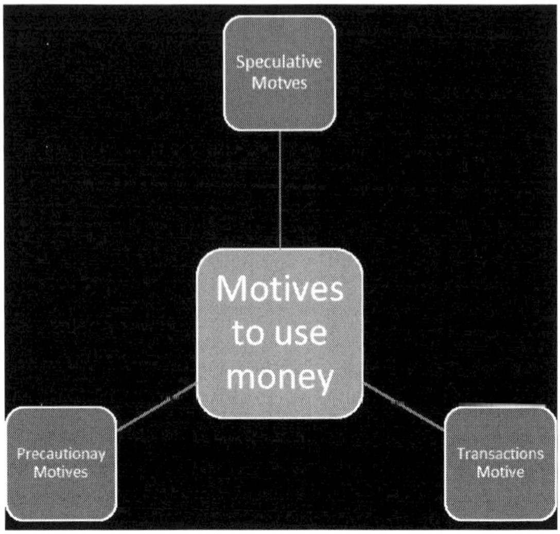

Figure 2.7: Motives to use money.

There are three broad motives based on which money is required by people, which are as discussed in subsection.

2.7.1. Transaction Motive

It relates to the demand for money to satisfy the current needs of individuals and businesses. On one hand, individuals need money to satisfy their prevailing requirements, which is known as income motive. On the other hand, businesses need money for the sole purpose of conducting their business activities, which is known as a business motive.

Transaction motive has two motives of money that are discussed below:

- **Income Motive:** It refers to the motive of individuals whose demand for money is to satisfy his/her basic needs or fulfilling the demands of their families. Generally, individuals hold cash for bridging the gap between the receipt of income and its eventual disbursement.

This is indeed a fact that the income an individual receives is once per month but the expenditure takes place every day. Therefore, it is necessary to hold some part of the income to make current payments on goods and services. The holding amount relies on the amount of an individual's income and the interval of receiving income.

- **Business Motive:** It refers to the requirement of money by businesses in liquid form to meet its current requirements.

Businesses require money for covering transport charges and procuring raw material, daily wages of labor, salaries, and other expenses. The demand for money by businesses depends on their turnover. The higher turnover means a higher amount of money to cover up business expenses.

2.7.2. Precautionary Motive

It refers to the desire of individuals to save extra money in case of future contingencies. These contingencies may include any mishappening such as sickness or accidents, sudden unemployment, and many more. The amount of money that an individual needs to save depends on the precautionary motive on the nature of a person and his/her living conditions.

2.7.3. Speculative Motive

It refers to the motive of individuals to save cash for future benefits from the movements of the market regarding the change in the interest rate or any investment opportunity that arises later on. The precautionary and speculative motive acts as the store of value for different purposes.

2.8. SUPPLY OF MONEY

As stated earlier, the demand for money is a demand for money to hold. Likewise, the supply of money refers to the supply of money to hold. Money does not exist if it is not held by individuals. Supply of money refers to the whole amount of money and it could be in any form that is held by a community in a given time.

Earlier, the most common form of money that constituted the major part of the money in an economy was metallic money. However, in this contemporary era, currency notes and checkable bank deposits have replaced metallic money.

The money supply is labeled as M1, M2, M3, and M4. M1 describes money stocks that comprise demand deposits, coins, and currency notes. M2 implies money stocks that comprise time deposits, currency notes, coins, and demand deposits.

M3 describes money stocks that comprise post office deposits, time deposits, currency notes, coins, and demand deposits. M4 states the money stock that comprises term deposits, saving banks, post office deposits, demand deposits, lime deposits, currency notes, and coins. The total supply of money is determined by the credit-control policies which are further imposed by the banking system of a country.

2.9. HOW BIG MONEY CORRUPTS THE ECONOMY

If politics is a war in other means, political spending is an economic war by other means. A fair political system is not affected by lobbying and runaway campaign spending. However, they only stand in the way of an economy that works for the middle class.

Specifically, why do super-rich and corporations drain their money into campaigns and lobbying? Sometimes politics comes into the playfield. But so far, more than small-scale donors, the most influential senders are investing in favorable policy outcomes.

Money not only gives a platform for big spenders to express a view or support a candidate, but it also provides the leverage to reshape the American economy in their possession (Figure 2.8).

Figure 2.8: Bribe is one of the most illegally done activities with money.

Source: Image by Needpix.

Also, the richest have been pulled away from the rest of America, the policies they desire are remarkably low tax rates on the wealthy at a tie of unchecked underinvestment in our future, special treatment for corporations and record deficits that are imposing major financial risk and environmental costs on our society. It is increasingly at odds with the policies that the country instantly needs.

It is indeed a fact that the money has always been a part of American politics. William McKinley's political fixer, Mark Hanna, once famously said, "There are two things that are important in politics. The first is money, and I can't remember what the second one is."

At the end of an era, Hanna spoke of the Gilded Age of staggering inequality and government corruption. In the following decades, reformers acted on the calls of Franklin Roosevelt ("we now know that the government by organized money is as dangerous as government by organized mob") and Theodore Roosevelt stated that ("the supreme political task of this day is to drive the special interests out of our public life") to reinvigorate a realm of civic life distinct from the inequalities and imbalances of the market.

The main purpose was not just the greater political equality, but it was also to restrict the capture of government by powerful economic interests and to build space for economic policies that would be in the interest of broad majorities of citizens.

Newer rules for Wall Street limited helped to avoid the destabilizing financial crises that were endemic under the hands of regime demanded by the financial industry.

Presenting economic security and a safer workplace meant workers were more productive and better protected. Increasing taxes on the heavily funded investments in education and infrastructure further provide long term advantages to society and the economy alike.

Nowadays, however, the floodwall between the democracy and market is vanishing away, and both sides of the barrier are being reshaped by the new flow of influence. Sheer volume of dollars is not just the reason that's driving the big change.

At least as important is the distance growing between the American population and those at the authoritative height of our economy and the rest of the Americans. The percentage of pre-tax national income going to the richest 0.1% has roughly been quadrupled since the 1970s. Simultaneously, as our economy has grown more globalized and finance has also increased in value. Most importantly, many rich companies have increasingly separated themselves from the prospect of common U.S. workers. The interests of today's corporate giants are not as quite aligned with the interests of the American middle class as they were ages ago.

The outcomes of these growing divides are clearly visible looming around us. A moderate response to the housing and job crisis even as Wall Street saw a large rescue, a recovery that's been much better for the richest 1% (who gained 93% of pre-tax income gains in 2010) than the rest of Americans; and rate of unemployment and joblessness remains tragically high.

Over the last generation, the middle class has faced stagnating opportunities for advancement, increasing health and education costs, and weakened job and retirement security. Despite this, the government has too often failed to respond, or their way of response has made the problem worse. An important reason is the weakening political clout of the common man in a more money centered political world.

2.9.1. Formal Regulation of Political Finance

To pass law and regulations are the two most common ways to address undesirable Behavior relating to money in politics. Rules on disclosure (financial reporting) aim to achieve transparency.

Bans and limits are the two aspects that directly aim to eliminate some specific types of Behavior. Public funding is often given to diminish the dependency of political parties and their candidates on private money. There are also many other forms of political finance regulations.

Rules that restrict the period during which campaign funds can be spent by establishing an official campaign period and rules relating to the abuse of state resources and media are some of the examples of such practices. Whatever rules are chosen, they must be suitable for the situation and goals of each country.

2.9.2. Disclosure

The availability of knowledge about political actors' finances, especially those of candidates and political parties is a major element in any effective system of the political finance control setup.

Lacking such significant knowledge, it is often next to impossible to know whether other forms of regulations are being respected. Transparency in the political finance, the setup has been established by the United Nations Convention against Corruption (UNCAC), which is a globally accepted responsible tool for the elimination of corruption.

It states that all the countries should "consider taking appropriate administrative and legislative measure, consistent with the objectives of this Convention and in accordance to the fundamental principles of its domestic law, to enhance the clarity in the funding of candidatures for elected public office and, wherever applicable in the funding of the political parties."

However, this is not the case as not many countries have introduced such rules and regulations because having such rules necessitates reporting which does not necessarily mean that the reports which are submitted are accurate or the reports are thoroughly audited.

While designing a disclosure system several considerations have to be taken into account for the political actors. The system must be perfect for every situation in each country. For instance, the system would account for how well established is the banking system and the capacity of political parties and candidates to comply.

Rules of financial reporting must not be too much complicated that stakeholders are not able to understand and abide by them. On the contrary, it is widely debated that public disclosure can make donors less willing to provide funds to the opposition parties and their candidates, thereby increasing the advantage of incumbency.

This must be weighed against the rights of the electorate to know about the financial dealing of those who may wish to represent their money flow to sustain transparency.

2.10. BANS AND LIMITS ON CONTRIBUTION AND EXPENDITURE

Sometimes, there is an argument that as long as the finances of electoral candidates and political parties are open and transparent, there is no need for further regulation.

The idea behind this theory is that the electorate will make its own decisions and that too depends on the information provided to them. For example, if a party is spending large amounts on gifts, the electorate may punish this populist approach by refusing to re-elect the party in the future. However, with given understanding, such an approach may not be effective everywhere and there is a reason to believe that. Where the media does not enjoy complete freedom or where the gap in access to funds is large, it becomes difficult for political finance to circulate information to get to the electorate (Figure 2.9).

Figure 2.9: Money laundering is a major concern in the political setup and crimes related to it.

Source: Image by The Blue Diamond Gallery.

In such circumstances, regulations are expected to make a move and target the Behavior of candidates and political parties. Also, not only to make the information available about such Behavior. Implementing bans is perhaps the only way to counter this undesired Behavior.

These bans can result in huge benefits as it may help to prevent political actors from receiving funds from "undesirable" sources, such as foreigners. The International IDEA database on political finance regulations declares that 70% of the 161 countries whose data was available thus, banned contributions from foreign sources.

According to some reports, few countries have also banned corporations from contributing to campaigns. The probable cause justified for this is that the corporations may be able to have an unfair influence on the Behavior of political actors. In the year of 2011, 22% of the 164 countries who hold the data were banned for such contributions. Implementing a ban on contributions from public funds, except for regulated provisions of public funding, is the only one way of offsetting the abuse of state resources. Many countries have implemented bans on anonymous donations and the reason behind is that if such donations are allowed, it becomes nearly impossible to verify whether bans on, and for example, foreign or corporate donations are upheld.

As per the IDEA database, 68% of the 152 countries whose data is available use a complete ban or a specific limit for anonymous donations, presenting it the most common type of contribution ban. If bans are imposed on expenditures then it can target obvious vices such as bribing election officials or vote-buying.

However, there is another theory to the mix as some countries also use bans to accomplish other goals; a good example could be leveling the playing field in election campaigns by banning activities like private advertising.

Bans imposed on advertising, also combined with the terms of free and equal access to print and broadcast media, and are sometimes viewed as a plan to limit the benefits of richer contestants. However, then comes to some critics that argue such rules may hinder free speech.

In these circumstances, countries may not desire to impose a ban on certain activities altogether. However, it may reduce them through the imposition of some limits. By Imposition, some limits to the amounts that people or companies can contribute, some countries wish to diminish the risk of large donations further influencing the decisions of politicians.

Such limits on contribution can also force candidates and political parties to target larger groups of people in their fundraising efforts. A change with the hope that it may enhance popular participation in politics. Limits can also be imposed based on money spent by candidates and political parties.

In many countries, the main motive behind imposing such limits is directed towards leveling the playing field between rich and poor contestants. However, limits can also serve to reduce overall spending on election campaigns and if it is studied, that such spending is excessive concerning the national economy or levels of poverty.

According to the data from the International IDEA, political finance database shows that around 30% of countries impose limits for any spending for political parties and 45% for candidates. Bans and limits on contributions and expenditure can serve as the only legit tool to control money in politics.

Nevertheless, there is hardly any point in introducing such regulations unless there is a functioning system of disclosure, including an effective

REFERENCES

1. Avis, E., Finan, F., Ferraz, C., & Varjão, C., (2017). *Money and Politics: The Effects of Campaign Spending Limits on Political Competition and Incumbency Advantage*. [eBook] National Bureau of Economic Research. Available at: https://www.nber.org/papers/w23508.pdf (accessed on 25 April 2020).
2. Beggs, J., (2018). *Why Not All Money is Created Equal*. [online] ThoughtCo. Available at: https://www.thoughtco.com/types-of-money-in-economics-1147762 (accessed on 25 April 2020).
3. Cliffsnotes.com. (n.d.). *Functions of Money*. [online] Available at: https://www.cliffsnotes.com/study-guides/economics/money-and-banking/functions-of-money (accessed on 25 April 2020).
4. Hacker, J., & Loewentheil, N., (2013). *How Big Money Corrupts the Economy*. [online] Democracy Journal. Available at: https://democracyjournal.org/magazine/27/how-big-money-corrupts-the-economy/ (accessed on 25 April 2020).
5. Investopedia. (2019). *Money Definition*. [online] Available at: https://www.investopedia.com/terms/m/money.asp (accessed on 25 April 2020).
6. Ohman, M., (2013). *Controlling Money in Politics: An Introduction*. [eBook] International Foundation for Electoral Systems. Available at: https://www.ifes.org/sites/default/files/a_brief_introduction_to_money_in_politics_final_magnus_ohman.pdf (accessed on 25 April 2020).
7. UKEssays.com. (2018). *Influence of Money and Media on Elections*. [online] Available at: https://www.ukessays.com/essays/politics/the-influence-of-money-and-media-on-politics.php (accessed on 25 April 2020).

Chapter 3

The Voting Systems and Politics

CONTENTS

The voting system and politics highlight the evolution of electoral process in different countries. In light, this article talks about the significance of voting system. A remarkable knowledge on how voting is the most important way to make your voice heard.

The decision is in the hands of public whether they want their country to progress or not. Otherwise, if people don't vote others will make the decisions for you. Briefly explained as to what electoral system is and how it is different in other countries.

Further, Legislative electoral systems have been explained with three different dimensions, i.e., plurality, and majority systems (collectively known as majoritarian systems), proportional systems, and hybrid or semi proportional systems.

At later stages, parliamentary systems, and presidential and semi-presidential system have been discussed. The article also gives the most key information about the privacy of voters in order to avoid bribed voting. Representation of woman and minorities has been discussed lately.

3.1. INTRODUCTION

An election may be described as a process in the political setup which makes it possible for the people to choose their preferences of a candidate for the political office or other position. The form and the context of elections are two different things and it is extremely important that there is a proper distinction among the two.

There are some cases, where the presence of the electoral forms is undeniable and is evident; however, there may be an absence of the substance of the elections. This can be seen in cases where the voters fail to get a proper choice, which may be considered free and genuine, among at least two candidates.

There are quite a lot of countries where the elections are carried out in some formal manner. However, there are countries where the election process does not guarantee competitiveness, which can be seen in the prohibition of any party to contest the elections except for one, or there may be cases where the kind of situation surrounding the elections is quite compromised to a great extent.

Over the last few years, network transactions for applications such as banking and Internet auctions have increased immensely. Moreover, network and mobile security technologies play an important role in protecting users' privacy.

In that regard, digital signatures got more eyeballs. Public-key cryptography enables a signer to sign a message using his or her private key, which is only owned by the signer, so that a digital signature can be brought up for the meant message. After that, any verifier can validate the correctness of this signature by using the signer's public key.

Nevertheless, it is appropriate to protect the privacy of signature receivers in certain kind of situations, which may be among the content of a message which has been signed and exists in a system of digital currency or may be a choice that has been taken from the candidates in an e-voting situation. David Chaum who was an expert in cryptology came up with a blind signature scheme in 1983 to offer blindness which protects the signee's privacy.

In 2013, Nayak et al. proposed a blind signature scheme based on an elliptic curve discrete logarithm problem. In 2005, Rabin introduced the concept of oblivious transfer. In 1994, Chen recommended that there must be a concept of random signatures known as oblivious signatures and that it must be of two kinds.

It was in the year 2008 that Tso and others proposed formal definitions for the oblivious signatures scheme and also recommended the security requirements for it. In 2012, Chou proposed a more decisive and secure out of oblivious transfer scheme.

In the year 1996, Mambo et al. proposed the concept of proxy signature. During this time, numerous proxy signature schemes have been proposed. In 2000, Lin, and Jan proposed the first proxy blind signature scheme that blends the functionalities of both proxy signatures and blind signatures.

In 2002, Tan et al. proposed a proxy blind signature scheme. However, in 2003, Lal, and Awasthi on being concerned about the insecurity of this scheme, proposed a new scheme replacing the old one, and most importantly it was secure and more effective than Tan et al.'s scheme. In 2013, Yang, and Liang proposed a new proxy blind signature scheme that allows revocation.

Ray and Narasimhamurthi came up with the idea of the electronic voting protocol which enables a voter to cast his or her ballot anonymously by exchanging undetectable authentic messages; this led to the evolution of electronic voting systems in 2001 (Figure 3.1).

Figure 3.1: Voting is a fundamental part of the political systems around the world.
Source: Image by PxHere.

Elections let us control who takes our decisions for us. In a democracy, we elect representatives to form policies for us. Policies at all levels are about allocating resources and prioritizing certain important things. Elections are one key way we choose to make these decisions.

In 2013, Pan et al. recommended an electronic voting scheme that truly works on the ring signature and is resistant to a clash attack. During the time, several schemes with delegated voting functionality have been proposed. In 2013, Zwattendorfer et al. proposed a proxy voting scheme that enables a voter to delegate his or her voting power to a proxy who casts the ballots for all represented voters.

Norway has utilized an Internet-based voting protocol for some years. Then, the scheme was demonstrated on its two key features, i.e., vote privacy and correctness. In the year 2016, Kulyk, and others recommended that there may be a novel proxy voting scheme which was resistant to coercion.

They did this by making a profound use of the JCJ/Civitas theme which was already resistant to coercion. This was done to try to keep direct voter coercion at bay and to keep away delegation coercion or any kind of proxy coercion.

They also recommended a new scheme of proxy-based voting as they incorporated the extension of Helios voting system which had the voting function in a delegated manner. Coming forward to 2017, Cohensius, and others focused on a problem arising out of social choice and reached to a conclusion that the voting system based on the proxy voting had the best proximity to the desired outcome.

3.2. DEFINITION OF VOTING SYSTEM

A voting system is not just the equipment mandatory to cast a vote. The voting system standards (VSS) have two different interpretations. First, addressing the two main functional and physical components of a voting system. Second, the physical aspect of voting system is a phenomenon comprising all the manuals, specifications, procedures, software, and hardware.

A discretionary framework or casting a ballot framework is a lot of throwing and preparing votes those capacities completely or incompletely by the utilization of electromechanical, or electronic mechanical assembly or by utilization of paper polling forms. However, it is not limited to the procedures for casting and processing votes. This comes up with a collaboration of tabulating cards, printouts, programs, operating manuals, and other software required for the system's operation.

Elections are a wholly process which let us figure out who makes our decisions for us. In a vote-based system like our own, we elect representatives to draft policies for us. Policy at every level is about distributing resources and ranking priorities. Elections are one key way we've decided to settle on these choices.

A voting system contains a set-up of specific procedures, hardware, and software components, and expendable supplies. It is configured into a system that allows votes to be cast and tabulated. It oversees how these elections are fairly conducted.

No single part of a democratic framework, for example, a precinct tabulation device, meets the real term of a voting system. Sufficient components must be assembled to make an arrangement, which will permit the framework all in all to meet all the necessities depicted for a democratic framework right now. The term electoral systems are, however, used to refer to a very specific catalog of norms and procedures which are generally employed in the elections to take a decision on the manner in which the persons responsible to hold decisive positions in a dispute, may be chosen.

Elections can be set apart from two particular points of view: the first one is identified with various levels of the political governance into which a nation may be classified such as that of national, state or district levels. Various candidates contest and get elected at these levels following different frameworks.

At the point when two extra components are viewed as the idea of the State (unitary or government) and the legislative system (unicameral or bicameral), the number of choices increments. A second fundamental contrast is the one identified with the way that positions in the debate might be single-or multi-member.

This differentiation is a vital keys to analyses the functioning and the performance of the systems of government. It oversees the link between the impacts delivered by the presidential and legislative elections are critical. Unfortunately, it will be limited to such a degree, that the most usually utilized meaning of discretionary frameworks is the most essential one: the interpretation of votes into seats.

If seen as a whole picture, there is a limit to the manner in which the various systems are present around the world for the purpose of the integration of the position pertaining to a single member.

In most cases, the winner in the elections, who is generally one person, among the other candidates, is selected, which may extend up to two persons I case that there is a vice-president to be selected besides a president on the same ticket.

When the election brings about the creation or renewal of a collegiate entity, the range of options is broadening. Also, its integration can be advised by different political objectives that are not necessarily reconcilable in practice.

While it is An important thing to ensure that there is a good amount of proportionality in the election process, there is also a significance of providing the party with more number of votes, a necessary number of seats so that they can form a majority in the parliament and can exercise their majority at the times of decision-making.

This provision may thus help them to govern in the way they desire, without needing an approval of the other parties which may be there in the opposition in the parliament. It is these two goals that have got the attention of the various scholars in the political field.

But they do not remain as the only goals that are followed or pursued by the political scholars when they sit down to design the various operations under the election procedure and the systems meant for it.

As it may be the case, the main reason pertaining to the creation of a proportional electoral system may not be a complex thing to achieve, it may be seen that having a government with majority of votes, can present genuine difficulties that could wind up forcing huge limitations for accomplishing the ideal target, not in light of the absence of regulatory or procedural instruments, but since its acknowledgment may require confused political courses of action.

In this way, the way toward designing and evaluating electoral systems to integrate collegiate entities can't open to a more extensive scope of potential outcomes, however, they have more instruments with extra variations that can make progressively complex its course of arrangement and operation.

3.2.1. What Electoral Systems Are?

At the most essential level, electoral systems interpret the votes cast in an election into results the offices/seats-won by parties and candidates.

The main factors impacting the electoral system formulation are:

- **The Electoral Formula:** This may be understood as a thing which decides the manner in which the seat is designated after an election depending on the majority of votes, or the proportionality of seats, or the kind of system used among mixed or any other ones available, or the mathematical formula.
- **The Ballot Structure:** This is to take a decision on whether a voter can vote for a single candidate for a certain seat or designation or the voter has to give their preferences for the series of candidates or parties.
- **The District Magnitude:** It is the number of representatives that are elected by the voters to represent their district and not the number of voters that reside in the district.

It must also be stressed on the fact that this topic of the area does not concentrate on the administrative aspects of elections (such as, the nomination of candidates who runs the elections, the registration of voters, the distribution of polling places, and so on) but in any case, these issues are of basic significance, and the potential favorable circumstances of some random electoral system decision can in some cases be undermined except if due consideration is paid to them. The designing of the electoral system also considers and emphasizes on the various other areas of the laws meant for electoral purposes.

This may be seen in the electoral system that is chosen by the authorities as it may have an impact on the manner in which the voters will be registered with the national agencies, or it may be seen in the way ballot papers are designed, the way in which the boundaries of various districts are determined, the manner of counting of votes or other kinds of considerations that are required in the electoral process.

The choice is one of the most significant institutional choices for any democracy. The decision of a specific constituent framework profoundly affects the future political existence of the nation concerned (Figure 3.2).

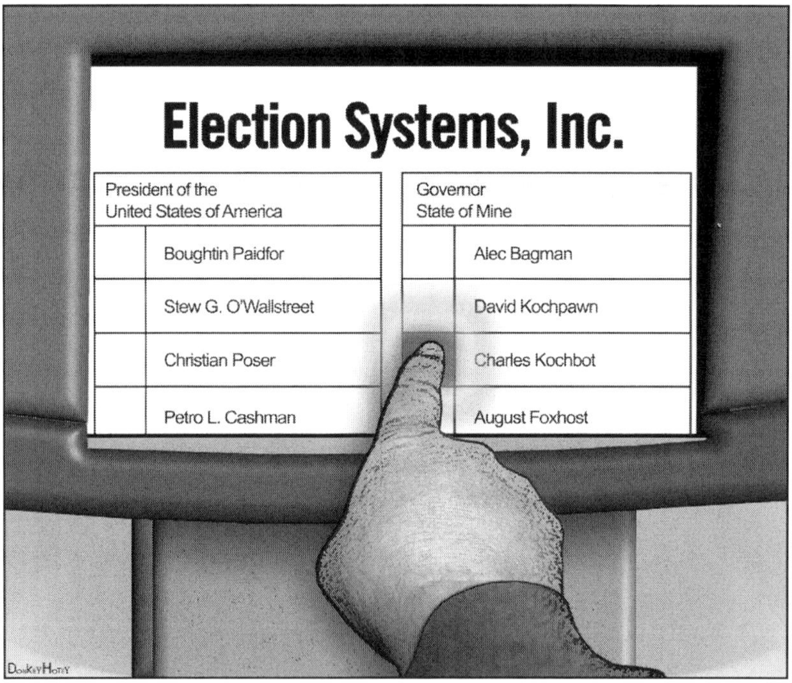

Figure 3.2: Election systems form an important entity in carrying out the elections.

Source: Image by Flickr.

In an electoral system, once chosen, they often remain fairly constant as political interests that set around and react to the motivations introduced by them. Be that as it may, while the conscious design has become undeniably increasingly predominant as of late, customarily it has been uncommon for electoral systems to be intentionally and purposely chose.

On quite a few occasions, it was an accidental choice which happened due to the mix-up of various kinds of circumstances or due to a certain trend which may just be passing by or may be determined by the way things happened in history as an outcome of the colonialism of the various parts of the world and the influence of neighbors often being especially strong.

Any new democracy is bound to choose (or inherit) an electoral system to elect its legislature. Equally, the political crisis within an established democracy may lead to a momentum for electoral system change. Even if it is without a political crisis, campaigners for political reform may attempt to put the electoral system change onto the political agenda.

Sometimes decisions may change keep in place, an electoral system is often affected by one of two circumstances which either political factors are lacking behind basic knowledge and information up to that extent so that the choices and consequences of different electoral systems are not fully recognized.

On the other hand there what matters is that how the people in the political circuit make use of the knowledge they have regarding the political setup so that they can vouch for the kind of political design which they consider good and appropriate for them to have an advantage in the elections.

Consequences largely loom where there is a decision taken in a dilemma that was unforeseen when they are introduced, as well as effects that were predicted. These decisions may not generally be the best ones for the long-haul political strength of the nation concerned, and now and again, they can have tragic ramifications for its democratic possibilities.

In the context of a choice of electoral system can be considered as important as the choice itself. Electoral system choice is a fundamentally political process, where independent technical experts can produce a single correct answer' putting aside to a big controversial question.

The thought of political favorable position is quite often a factor in the decision of electoral systems. Here and there, it is the main thought while the menu of accessible electoral systems decisions is regularly, in actuality, a generally compelled one.

Also, the estimations of transient political intrigue can frequently darken the more extended term outcomes of a specific discretionary framework and the interests of the more extensive electoral system. As an outcome, while perceiving the pragmatic limitations, this content endeavors to move toward the issue of electoral system decisions in as expansive and far-reaching a way as could reasonably be expected.

As the crafting of political institutions is an analytical task not only for new democracies but also for those well-established democracies that are seeking to adapt their systems for a better reflect new political realities.

This subject area primarily aims to throw light on the various possible concerns of the people belonging to the already settled democratic nations, who may be in charge of having the electoral systems redesigned and the people in those nations who may be taking part in the various debates focusing on the purposes and activities of the various political institutions in the democracies that are new and in their formative stages.

Given this intended interest group, a significant part of the scholastic writing regarding the matter is fundamentally disentangled, while simultaneously this content endeavors to address a portion of the more intricate issues inborn in the territory. In the event that the content has all the earmarks of being in some cases excessively short-sighted and at different occasions unduly unpredictable, the clarification, for the most part, lies in the endeavor to balance the two objectives of clarity and comprehensiveness.

While the framework in which emerging and established democracies make institutional choices that can fluctuate tremendously. The long-term intentions of the democracies are mostly about the creation of the foundations which can support the stability of the democracy in the advanced stages, and may also be able to adapt enough so that they can respond to the various conditions as the democracy evolves through time.

Learning process implements everywhere, and so in politics where each democracy learns from one another to grow. Institutional design is an evolving process, and this text seeks to distill the lessons learned from the many actual examples of institutional design around the world.

Between the 1980s and the 1990s, the movement of the world towards governing their nations in a democratic way gave rise to a new kind of urgency so that new models to represent the candidates can be searched by the institutions and the electoral systems can be evaluated afresh.

This thing has gone up by many margins at the starting of this century. The process as a whole was promoted by the thought and fact that there could be a huge impact on the whole political system depending on the choices made by the political institutions.

For example, it is progressively being perceived that an electoral system can be planned both to give neighborhood geographic portrayal and to advance the guideline of proportionality; can advance the improvement of solid and reasonable national political parties, and guarantee the portrayal of woman and provincial minorities, and can assist with designing' collaboration and convenience in a separated society by the innovative utilization of specific impetuses and limitations.

Electoral systems are today observed as one of the most influential of all political institutions, and crucial importance to broader issues of governing.

3.3. PROPERTIES OF VOTING SYSTEMS

Researchers in the electronic voting field have already reached a consensus pack of four crucial properties that an electronic voting system should have. According to Cranor and Cytron (1997), the voting protocol consists of the following (Figure 3.3):

1. Accuracy:

- A vote can't be altered.
- A vote which has been successfully validated can be removed from the final list.
- An invalid vote can't be counted in the final tally.

2. Democracy:

- In democracy, only the voters who are eligible get to vote.
- It has to be ensured that even the voters eligible to vote, vote only once.

3. Privacy:

1. It implies that no one can trace or link the vote cast by any voter to the ballot it has been cast in, including the authorities.
2. It also implies that no voter has the power t prove that they cast a certain vote.

3.3.1. Verifiability

It implies that all the people in the voting system have the authority to verify if the vote's cats have been cast independently or not.

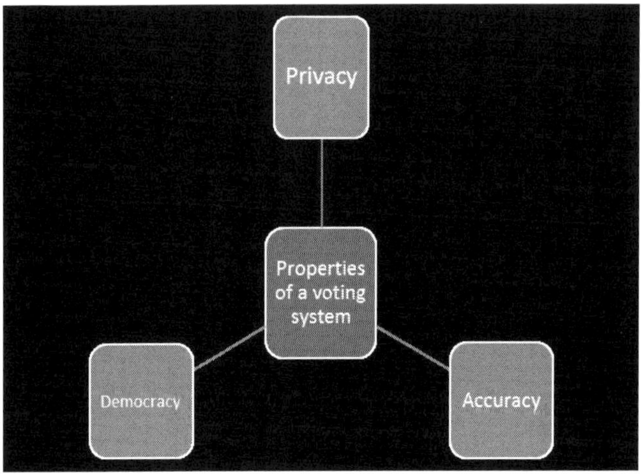

Figure 3.3: Properties of a good voting system.

Accuracy, democracy, and verifiability are, by, and large of the present electoral system, guaranteed by the present representatives of the opposite party. The protection property is as of now guaranteed by the presence of private voting booths, permitting voters to cast their votes in mystery.

3.4. SYSTEMS OF VOTE COUNTING

Individual votes are interpreted into aggregate choices by a wide assortment of rules of counting that the voters and leaders have acknowledged as authentic before the election. These guidelines may on a basic level call for majority casting a ballot, which requires just that the victor has the best number of votes.

The number of votes which were in excess of half the total number of votes cast. The extraordinary majority voting is a concept that requires the winner to have a higher proportion, such as a two-third majority. There is a concept of proportional voting which implies that is a political party is to be able to represent voters with unanimity, they need to receive a certain threshold of votes.

3.4.1. Legislative Elections

There are a lot of electoral systems that may be found to bring the legislative seats in proper proportion. The electoral systems can, however, be normally classified into three major kinds of classification systems:

- The plurality and majority systems which are together known as majoritarian systems;
- The proportional systems; and
- The hybrid systems which are also known as the semi-proportional systems.

The electoral system is a critical variable in clarifying open strategy choices since it decides the quantity of political parties ready to get portrayal and in this way take an interest in government.

3.4.2. Plurality and Majority Systems

The first kind of system, the plurality system, is one of the smoothest ways to come to a conclusion for the results of the election. If a candidate needs to win an election, they must ensure that they get a bigger number of votes than some other single adversary. As has been stated by the majority formula, a candidate does not need to have more votes polled for them than the total combined votes of the opposition.

The chances of the candidate who is winning the seat of a legislative place getting minority number of votes to win the seat go up as the number of candidates who are contesting from the seat goes up.

There are many countries that taken up the plurality formula to be applied in their national elections and these countries are among Canada, India, Great Britain, and the United States. It is usually found that the countries with the plurality electoral system have two main parties contesting for a seat.

As seen from the electoral system of majority, the party or the candidate is declared as a winner if they get votes in excess of 50% from a constituency. The issue in a system with the absolute majority measure is that it may not be fulfilled in challenges in which there are multiple candidates.

There have been various kinds of majority formula that have been brought up by the various scholars and political researchers so that they can address this problem. In the Australian country, in the elections taking place in the lower house, the preferential or the alternative voting system is used. Voters rank the candidates' position on an alternative-preference ballot.

In case that a majority cannot be reached by following the approach of first preference, then the weakest candidate is eliminated. The further procedure takes place by redistributing the votes of the voters as per their second or third preference that they have given in the ballot. This redistributive process is continuously repeated until one candidate has achieved a clear majority of the votes. In France, a double-ballot system is employed for the National Assembly elections. Another round will be taken into consideration in case no candidate secures a majority in the first round of elections.

In the second round, only those candidates securing the votes of at least one-eighth of the enrolled electorate in the first round may contend, and the candidate making sure about a majority of the mainstream vote in the second round is announced as the legitimate winner.

Some candidates are eligible for the second round to withdraw their candidacy and endorse it as one of the leading candidates. On the contrary, to the two-party rule of the plurality system, some analysts in France have called a two-bloc system.

It states that the main parties of the left and the main parties of the right go up against one another in the first round of an election to become the representative of their particular ideological group. At that point, they partner with each other to boost their alliance's portrayal in the second round.

There is an electoral system—the supplementary vote system-which is very rarely used and was brought into use at the London mayoral elections. As per this voting system, the voters are required to rank the two representatives they prefer. If there is no applicant who can win a majority in the first round of viewing the first preference, all polling forms not demonstrating the best two vote-getters as either a first or a subsequent option are disposed of.

The formula catering to the majority rule applies to only the electoral constituencies that have only one member in them. It is not always expected the majority or the plurality formulas are able to distribute the seats under legislature in the appropriate proportion to the vote share of the popularity of the competing candidates.

Both the formulas tend to give good returns to the strong party out of proportion, which in turn hurts the weaker part out of proportion too.

Although, these parties may escape from the inequities of the system if their support is regionally concentrated. For example, the 2001 national elections held in Britain culminated with the Labor Party captured more than three-fifths of the seats in the House of Commons.

Generally, the formula of plurality presents a more distorted image of the manner in which the seats have been distributed as compared to the majority system. However, it does not happen the same way always.

3.4.3. Proportional Representation (PR)

Proportional representation (PR) requires that the allocation of seats extensively be relative to the distribution of the well-known vote among contending political parties. It looks to overcome the disproportionalities that outcome from majority and plurality equations and to make a delegate body that mirrors the dispersion of assessment inside the electorate.

Due to the utilization of multimember constituencies in PR, parties with neither a majority nor a plurality of the famous vote can in any case win legislative representation. Considerably, the number of political parties that are represented in the governing body frequently is enormous. For example, in Israel, there are usually more than 10 parties in the Knesset.

Several factors can generate disproportional outcomes even under PR. The most important factor that holds major significance in deciding the actual extent of proportionality of the electoral system of proportionality is the district magnitude. District magnitude is the number of candidates that are elected by the voters from a single constituency.

The greater the electoral district has the number of seats in them, the more proportional the outcome will be. A second significant factor is a specific formula used to translate votes into seats. Single transferable vote and party-list PR is preferably known as the two basic types of formula.

3.4.4. Single Transferable Vote

It was during the time of the 19th century that the vote formula for the electoral system of single transferrable vote found its existence in Denmark and Britain. It is also known as the Hare system which was named after one of its British proponents of electoral reform, Thomas Hare. It employs a ballot that allows the voter to rank candidates in order of their preference.

At the point when the polling forms are tallied, any competitor accepting the fundamental amount of first inclination votes, determined as one or more the quantity of votes isolated by the quantity of seats in addition to one is granted a seat.

In the various kinds of computations that hold discretion, the votes secured by a candidate who is winning which are more than the share are moved to another candidate agreeing according to the preference they have given in the ballot as their second preference, which is held under the STV system. Any candidate who then accomplishes the necessary quota is also awarded a seat. This process is a recurring one, in which the votes in surplus are transferred to the remaining candidates until the remaining seats have found a candidate that can fit in. The best and the most optimal constituencies for the application of the single transferrable voting system is that of five members.

As the system involves the consideration of the preferences that have been ranked by the voters, the electoral system of single transferrable vote involves a lot of complex computations. This complexity coupled with the fact that its use minimizes the impact of the political parties on the elections, limits its use.

It has been used in Northern Ireland and Malta and the selection of the Australian and South African senates. The main advantage of the Hare formula is that it lays a lot of emphasis on the candidates and not on the parties that may belong to, which makes it unique among all.

The party affiliation of the candidates doesn't matter to the calculations. The accomplishment of minor parties fluctuates extensively, little anti-extremist gatherings for the most part profit by the vote moves, however, small extremist parties typically are punished.

Party-List Proportional Representation (PR)

The single transferable vote formula and list system has a basic point of difference among them which finds its significance in the various elections that are conducted in the Western Europe and Latin America. This difference is that in the list system, the voters have the option to choose the candidate from the list that has been compiled by the party, indicating the candidates party-wise, and not go just for the list of individual candidates to select from.

However, the voters may have some limited options among individual candidates, electoral computations are made based on party affiliation, and seats are awarded based on party rather than the total number of candidates.

The allocation of the seats that have been won by the party is done by the manner in which the candidates appear on the list that was proposed by the party. In the electoral systems, there are several kinds of formulas that are employed. However, the main two types of formulas are:

- Largest average formula; and
- Greatest remainder formula.

As per the formula of the largest average, the seats are awarded to the candidates one by one and the candidates are from the party that has got the largest average number of votes.

The average number of votes is calculated by dividing the total number of votes that have been secured by the party by the total number of seats that have been awarded to the party and to this number an integer is added which generally depends on the method that has been adopted for the calculation,

Each time a party wins a seat, the divisor for that party increases by the same integer which further diminishes its odds of winning the following seat. Under all strategies, the first seat is granted to the gathering with the biggest absolute number of votes, since, no seats having been assigned, the normal vote aggregate as dictated by the equation will be biggest for this party.

The greatest-remainder method first set up a quota that is important for a party to receive representation. Formulas vary, but they have generally some variation of dividing the total vote in the district by the number of seats.

The total popular vote won by each party is partitioned by the portion, and a seat is granted the same number of times as the gathering all out contains the full share. In the event that all the seats are granted right now, political race is finished. However, such fallout is unlikely to take place.

Seats that are not won by full standards accordingly are granted to the parties with the biggest rest of votes after the share hosts been subtracted from each get-together's all out decision in favor of each seat it was granted. Seats are circulated consecutively to the gatherings with the biggest leftover portion until all the region's designated seats have been granted.

The small parties generally tend to manage their allocations and elections better when they follow the greatest-remainder formula as compared to when they follows the largest average formula. The greatest-remainder formula is used in Israel and Luxembourg and for some seats in the Danish Folketing.

Before 1994, Italy utilized an uncommon variation of the best leftover portion equation, called the Imperial formula, whereby the constituent quantity was set up by isolating the complete famous vote by the quantity of seats in addition to two. This change expanded the authoritative portrayal of little gatherings however, it prompted a more noteworthy twisting of the corresponding perfect.

The proportionality of results likewise can be weakened by the inconvenience of an appointive edge that requires an ideological group to surpass some base level of the vote to get representation.

3.4.5. Hybrid Systems

In some countries, the majoritarian and proportional systems are consolidated into what is known as blended part corresponding or extra individual's system. Despite the fact that there are a few variations, all blended part corresponding systems choose a few agents by relative portrayal (PR) and the rest of a non-corresponding equation.

One of the main points of difference between the mixed-member systems is the proportion or the percentage in which the seats are allocated under the proportional methods and the majoritarian methods. For example, in Italy and Japan, respectively, roughly three-fourths and three-fifths of all seats are apportioned through constituency elections.

The way in which a nation chooses the electoral system it wants is reflected in the particular kind of culture they follow, the circumstances that they have been with regard to society, politics, and their history, which is similar to the way the conception of their representation comes up. A large number of plural methods of voting have the best possibility of being acceptable in political cultures that are relatively stable.

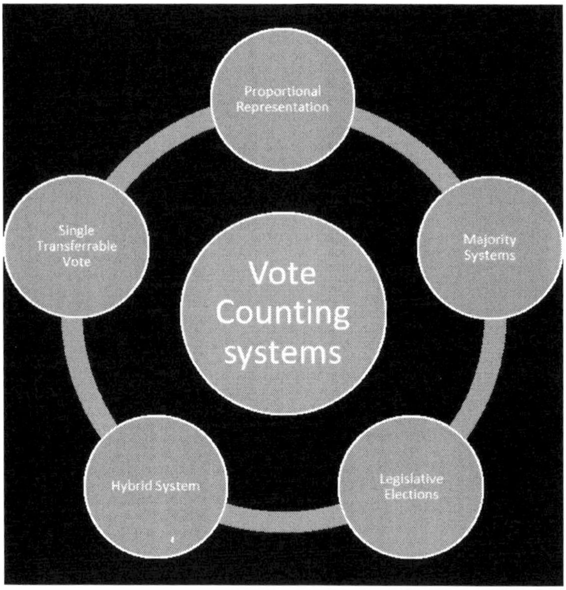

Figure 3.4: Various systems of counting the votes.

In such cultures, fluctuations in electoral support from one election to the next to reduce polarization and encourage political centrism. Thus, the winner takes all implications of the majority or plurality formulas are not experienced as unduly derivational or restrictive.

On the contrary, in societies with traditional ethnic, linguistic, and religious inclinations or in societies that have experienced class and ideological conflict is where PR is more likely to be found (Figure 3.4).

3.5. EXECUTIVE ELECTIONS

3.5.1. Parliamentary Systems

Although, some members still manage to attain their position by heredity, most are now elected. In most parliamentary systems, the head of government is elected by the legislature.

Inferable from the unexpected further chipping of the political framework, however, officials later casted a ballot to re-establish their job in choosing the head administrator. Parliamentary frameworks that have, notwithstanding a head administrator, a less-amazing nonhereditary president have embraced various techniques for his political race.

For example, in Germany, the president is selected by both the upper and the lower chamber of the legislature. On the contrary, rules are different in Ireland; the president is elected by a plurality vote of the public.

3.5.2. Presidential and Semi-Presidential Systems

In presidential systems and mixed (semi-presidential) systems, the head of state is elected independently by the legislature. Several methods of electing presidents have been adopted in the past.

The synthesis of the Electoral College, which chooses the president, is controlled by a majority vote taken inside each state.

Although voters decide between the various presidential candidates, they are in effect choosing the electors who will elect the president using a majority vote in the Electoral College.

3.6. WHAT DO VOTING SYSTEM STANDARDS (VSS) ADDRESS?

Each state lays down its specific standards for voting systems in statute or administrative rule. These can be based on the voluntary standards set by the EAC, or not. The most common issues that VSS are likely to encounter are privacy, usability, accessibility security, and functionality,

3.6.1. Security

A secure voting machine is something which cannot be tampered with or manipulated. This is a necessity to avoid unauthorized alteration. Security begins with requiring that systems accurately record votes as cast. Although requirements vary from state to state, other aspects of security that may be addressed include:

1. **Physical Security of the Equipment and Ballots:** It is a procedure that ensures that additional votes cannot be cast after the polls have closed or tampered with at any stage of the process and that there is an auditable chain of custody.
2. **Auditability:** The capability of a machine to maintain an audit record that can be reviewed post-election.
3. **Internet Connection:** Ensuring a machine cannot be connected to the Internet or networked during the voting period to avoid the potential for hacking.
4. **Functionality:** Standards may also address specific functionality that a voting machine should have. Functionality might include:

i. Correctly registering and recording all votes cast.
ii. Permitting the voter to vote for any person, office, or measure for which he or she has the right to vote.
iii. Permitting a voter to review his or her votes before casting them. Also, providing the opportunity to change or correct the ballot before it is cast and counted.
iv. Notifying a voter if he or she has cast too many votes for a particular candidate or issue (over voted) or neglected to vote for a particular candidate or issue (undervote).
v. Providing a method for voters to write-in a candidate of their choice.
vi. Accumulating total ballots cast.

3.6.2. Privacy

Voters have a legal right to a secret ballot and to cast their votes in private. This is necessary to protect voters from being coerced or bribed into voting a certain way. In the context of a voting machine, this means that the system shouldn't provide a receipt or any way for another person to determine the contents of a voter's ballot.

3.6.3. Usability

Casting a ballot should be easy for voters. This means that a voting machine should be as intuitive to use as possible and contain clear instructions regarding how to vote. The way that the ballot is designed and presented either on-screen or on paper is also important. Ballot design and usability is an integral part of voting system design.

3.6.4. Accessibility

By federal law, all people, including those with visual, physical, or cognitive disabilities, must have the opportunity to independently cast their votes. Paper is not accessible for many people, either because of vision impairment or because pen and paper are hard to manipulate.

As the population ages, the demand for adaptive systems continues to grow. By federal law, voting systems must also have the ability to provide alternative language accessibility (Figure 3.5).

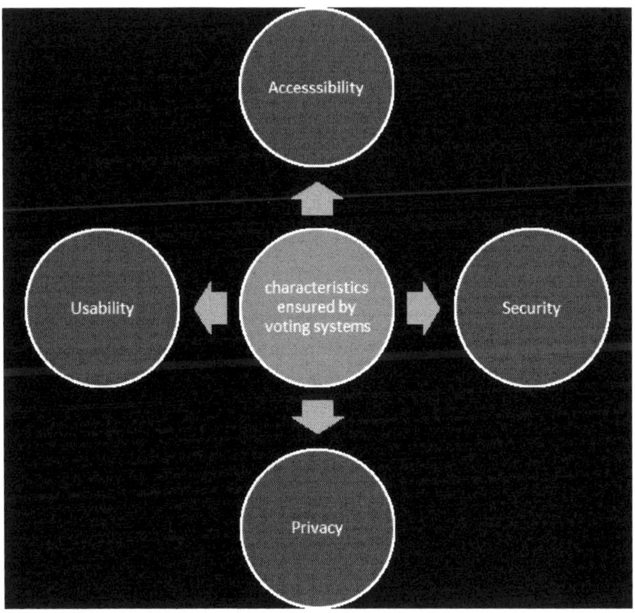

Figure 3.5: Things addressed by voting systems.

3.7. CRITERIA FOR DESIGNING

While designing an electoral system, it is best to proceed with a list of criteria that sum up what you want to achieve, what you want to avoid and, in a broad sense, what you want your legislature and executive government to look like.

It is the idea of institutional plan that exchange offs must be made between a few contending wants and destinations. These documents center essentially around criteria for the frameworks and not on the structure procedure itself. The structure procedure is canvassed in more profundity in the areas Process of Change and Advice for Electoral Systems Designers.

For instance, one might need to permit free contender to be chosen, and simultaneously to empower the development of solid political groups. Or on the other hand, discretionary systems creators may figure it astute to make a framework that gives voters a wide level of decision among applicants and gatherings.

Be that as it may, this may make for a confused voting form paper which causes challenges for less-taught voters. The stunt in picking (or transforming) a constituent system is to organize the criteria that are generally significant and afterward evaluate which discretionary framework, or mix of frameworks, best amplifies the fulfillment of these destinations.

3.8. POLITICAL CONSEQUENCES OF THE ELECTORAL SYSTEM

3.8.1. Proportionality

One of the major topics of discussion (and cause of disagreement among scholars) is how the electoral system affects the proportionality. How proportional is a PR system (henceforth referred to as PR)?

The question may sound very simple; however, this is not the case. Three independent variables are explaining the degree of proportionality, which are discussed here: district magnitude, the ballot structure, and electoral formulae.

There are general agreements about the significance of district magnitude. The larger the number of seats in the constituency the more proportional is the system (Rae, 1967; Lijphart, 1994).

Sometimes it is viewed as another dimension of this variable is the electoral threshold:

- Largest remainder-Hare; Saint-Laguë.
- Largest remainder-Droop; STV; modified Saint-Laguë.
- D´Hondt; largest remainder-Imperial.

3.8.2. Representation of Women

Different type of electoral system is considered to be the most significant predictor while having women's parliamentary recruitment, even when it is compared with socio-economic variables like education and income.

According to several studies, the list-PR system provides the most political opportunity for women to take place in parliament (Lovenduski and Norris, 1993; Rule, 1987). In western democracies, the proportion of women parliamentarians is increasing, and the greatest increase being in proportional systems (Norris, 1996).

3.8.3. Representation of Minorities

The electoral system can also influence the way ethnic, linguistic, and religious minorities are represented in so-called heterogeneous societies. In a plural-majority system, minorities are rarely able to muster enough votes to get their representatives elected.

Proportional system, then again, lessens the impact of the predominant gatherings and political gatherings and award minorities a method for access to the political stage by promising them some proportion of portrayal.

Proportional system along these lines gives a more genuine image of society. The utilization of relative democratic as a method for making sure about portrayal for minorities' goes back to the times of the French Revolution.

Proponents of the system incorporated the British scholar John Stuart Mill, who accepted that it may secure the interests of ethnic and semantic minorities in the new national states, when such gatherings were truly undermined by the control of the larger part.

3.8.4. Party Systems

Another important outcome of the electoral system is the effect on the number of parties. The connection between the non-proportional system and

3.10. CONCLUSION

To conclude, we get to know about what electoral systems are. This article clearly stated the meaning of democracy. The choice of the Electoral System is one of the most important institutional decisions for any democracy.

According to Cranor and Cytron 1997 voting protocol, we learned about the properties of voting system. The privacy property is currently assured by the existence of private voting booths, allowing voters to cast their votes in secrecy.

This article briefly talked about the VSS as a secure voting machine will ensure fair game play and avoid being tampered with or manipulated. This is a necessity to avoid unauthorized alteration.

This article also stated that the Elections can be set apart from two distinct perspectives: the first one is related to the different levels of government in which a country is divided (national, state, or local level). A second essential difference is the one related to the fact that positions in dispute may be single- or multi-member.

REFERENCES

1. Aceproject.org. (n.d.). *Electoral Systems.* [online] Available at: https://aceproject.org/ace-en/topics/es/onePage (accessed on 25 April 2020).
2. Assembly.coe.int. (2000). *Impact of Electoral Systems on the Political Process.* [online] Available at: http://assembly.coe.int/nw/xml/XRef/X2H-Xref-ViewHTML.asp?FileID=9090 (accessed on 25 April 2020).
3. Chiou, S., Wang, T., & Chen, J., (2017). Design and implementation of a mobile voting system using a novel oblivious and proxy signature. *Security and Communication Networks*, [online], pp. 1–16. Available at: https://www.hindawi.com/journals/scn/2017/3075210/ (accessed on 25 April 2020).
4. Encyclopedia Britannica, (n.d.). *Election-Executive Elections.* [online] Available at: https://www.britannica.com/topic/election-political-science/Executive-elections (accessed on 25 April 2020).
5. Ncsl.org. (2018). *Voting System Standards, Testing and Certification.* [online] Available at: https://www.ncsl.org/research/elections-and-campaigns/voting-system-standards-testing-and-certification.aspx (accessed on 25 April 2020).
6. UKEssays.com. (2016). *Definition of Voting System Information Technology Essay.* [online] Available at: https://www.ukessays.com/essays/information-technology/definition-of-voting-system-information-technology-essay.php (accessed on 25 April 2020).

Chapter 4

Judiciary, Politics, and Crime

CONTENTS

As seen, the crime in politics is a major area of concern for the stakeholders, especially the people for which the government is acting. As crimes rise in politics or elsewhere, the judiciary assumes a great deal of importance to combat the crimes or to punish the criminals so that justice can be served to the victims.

This chapter makes the readers aware about the various aspects of the judiciary and how it acts to make criminal justice available readily. The chapter also emphasizes on the importance of the judiciary to instill faith in the people and to check the criminal activities taking place in the political systems.

4.1. INTRODUCTION

Dictionary meaning of the word Judiciary is 'the system of courts of justice in a country.' Judiciary is that part of government or central authority in a country which has the authority to interpret and apply the law, take decision or make formal judgments' for any legal disputes and administer justice.

Judiciary handles the cases when any dispute results in litigation. The litigants or parties to the lawsuit could be individuals, groups, legal entities (e.g., partnership or corporation) or governments and agencies (Figure 4.1).

Figure 4.1: Judiciary is a key player in the political systems.

Source: Image by Wikimedia Commons.

Civil cases involve conflicts when people (individual or group) or institutions claims that someone has done something illegal or wrong (could be personal or financial) resulting from violations of law. The two parties in civil cases are 'the plaintiff' (i.e., the person who files the case) and 'the defendant' (i.e., the person against whom the case is filed).

Usually, in civil cases, the losing party pays financial compensation to the one who wins the case. Crimes give rise to criminal cases. Criminal cases are a case where the conflict is between the State or its citizens and the defendant, which means the person is charged with having committed or omitted an act against the state or society.

In criminal cases, if the person (or defendant) who committed the crime is found guilty, the defendant is sentenced to punishment and may have to pay fine, serve time in jail, or in matters that are very serious, the punishment could also involve state-imposed physical mutilation or death.

The judiciary is the system of courts that interprets and applies the law in the name of the state. The judiciary can also be thought of as the mechanism for the resolution of disputes.

Administrative cases are cases involving disputes between State or Government agencies on one side and the individuals, groups or legal bodies on the other. Disputes in case of Administrative cases are pertaining to rules, regulations, and procedures of a State agency.

Judiciaries look after administrative cases as well. Any government of State may not be sued by any non-state litigants without their prior consent according to the principle of state sovereignty incorporated by most legal systems.

This surely put a limit to litigant's right to seek take action against government or State bodies. However, administrative cases handle many such cases to protect citizen's right and looks after the cases that involve irrational, irregular, and abusive application of laws and government rules and regulations.

The process to interpret and enforce the law depends on the extent to which the courts judiciaries can handle the cases. There are few courts that take charge of all civil, criminal, and administrative cases at one place. And then some courts are specialized civil, criminal, and administrative courts. There are also, few who handle general and some specialized cases as well.

Sometimes, the disputes or the conflicts are uncontested, which means such cases are settled without going to trial. Examples are civil cases like uncontested divorce, child custody dispute, interpretation of agreements/ contracts, etc.

However, in US, a lot of criminal cases too have uncontested dismissal where the cases are settled by extrajudicial plea bargain instead of jury trial. Varied criminal process in the United Kingdom and civil-law countries makes uncontested dismissal or plea bargaining of the sort in the United States impossible.

In a country like Germany, guilty plea or plea bargaining in case of criminal trials is unknown whereas in the UK, like the US, similar practices of plea bargaining are prevalent.

In plea bargaining or negotiating a plea cases, the court's role is limited to administrative. In the absence of trial and out of court settlement, the court just needs to officially validate and record the conclusion (or agreement) between the parties and the case gets closed.

When the judiciary believes that, there exists a disagreement or dispute between the parties, the regulatory body administers the rules like-what is allowed before the court, what evidence to be submitted, trial procedure to be followed, and the type of judgments that may be pronounced or declared.

A number of people are involved in the judicial proceedings. When the trial proceeding begins, apart from the judge who is the central figure and people or entities who are directly involved in a lawsuit (i.e., Parties) and their respective lawyers, other individuals involved are witnesses, clerks, bailiffs, administrators, and jurors.

The explicit function of the courts is to make a formal judgment about a disputed matter over the application of laws in certain cases. However, courts also make law and public policy. Judges exercise some discretion to pass the judgment after hearing both the parties in favor of litigant whose claims are within the legal boundaries and more appropriate once they hear both the parties.

The powerful national supreme courts (as in the US, Germany, and India) have the power to abolish any laws, statutes, regulations, or government actions that violate the Constitution of the country. Lawmaking and policymaking is not only limited to above.

Judiciaries exercise the discretionary power when they are acting as administrators even for validating the interpretation of contracts, where cases are settled without going to trial.

It is usually seen that the suits between employers and employees work in favor of employees because they are influenced by de facto changes in the law that may result from the decisions by juries or trial judges who may regularly be more sympathetic to workers.

Formal laws (i.e., the law which is passed by state legislature, then made into a statue by giving it a number in the right chapter) can also be altered from time to time in cases like child custody, financial settlement in divorce cases.

Once the court has passed the judgment, enforcement may or may not be required. There are cases where both the parties respect court's decision. However, there are few cases; a court passes the order to the party to stop a particular activity.

Usually, the legislative branch does the funding in such cases and the orders are carried out by the executive branch. It is said that the courts (or judiciary) possess neither the power of the sword nor the power of the purse.

Hence, the judiciary is known to be the least dangerous branch of government. In reality, enforcement of the orders of any government institution depends on the enforcing institution's acceptance of the issuing institution's right to make the ruling and to have it enforced.

4.2. THE CONCEPT OF JUDICIAL INDEPENDENCE

As the term 'judicial independence' denotes it means that, the judiciary should be independent from the other branches of government. The role of judicial independence in a liberal republican democracy is to protect political and civil rights and also the rule of law.

There are three most significant components of the Judiciary. The very first is utility, and efficiency. For this, courts must be useful to its people where court is expected to lawfully punish the culprit, protect civil rights and privileges, and justly resolve disputes.

Court is also expected to be efficient in all their work, thereby not causing any waste and delay, as this would result in less political support. Insulation and accountability are the second component (Figure 4.2).

Figure 4.2: The decisions taken by the judges have a great impact on the political consequences of a state.

Source: Image by Flickr.

This means that the courts are politically insulated to the executive, legislature, and political parties. Also, no social, economic, or political power can influence the court's decision. Moreover, the court is accountable for its actions and decisions to the laws, constitution, and its people.

Lack of accountability will take away the public's trust towards the courts and will encourage other political bodies to take an advantage of unaccountability and exercise its control. Authority and restraint are the last components.

The decisions of the court not only carry legal but moral authority. Court is the judicial branch of the government holding the judicial authority and the ability to enforce their decisions and orders.

The correct use of judicial authority brings the trust and confidence in other institutions as well. At the same time, courts must limit the use of their power to abolish any laws or announce them unfair unless there is a conflict with the constitution (Figure 4.3).

Figure 4.3: The political systems of various states are run by the judiciary of that system.

Source: Image by Wikimedia Commons.

The judiciary independence also means that the judges can independently construe and apply the laws freely and fairly, being impartial and objective and not subject to undue pressure from the other branches of government, police, military, public opinion or any other government bodies or individuals.

In order to have this judiciary independence in practice, judges are appointed for long term, sometimes even for lifetime and is difficult to remove the judges. Usually, the term 'judicial independence' is referred to in a normative sense to indicate what type of independence is expected out of the judges and the courts.

Hence, there lies confusion over the meaning of the term 'Judicial Independence,' since one is totally based on concept and the other one is normative. In the conceptual meaning, there is a lack of clarity on the kind of independence, courts, and judges are capable of possessing while in case of normative, the form of disagreement over what type of independence courts and judges must possess.

It is important to be logical, consistent, and comprehensive here and hence the judicial independence must answer the questions like-independence for whom, independence from him, and independence for what and independence for what purpose. In the United States, the federal government gives all members of the Supreme Court, District court and the appeal court lifetime tenure. The other federal judges get substantial term like fifteen years for the judges of bankruptcy courts. The selection of the proper judiciary is another point in judicial independence.

The American Bar Association supports the selection of the judges on the basis of clearance by screening committee. This process of selection is also called merit selection. However, many state legislatures advocates election of judges by the general public.

Judicial election is seen more as rewarding political skills than legal skills by the American Bar Association and the State Bar Association. In 2000, for the case of Bush V. Gore, the focus was on the judicial outcomes instead of the traditional focus on judicial qualifications.

4.3. THE MANY MEANINGS OF "POLITICS" IN JUDICIAL DECISION MAKING

There is no doubt that the role of politics in judicial decision making is one of the hot topics of discussion today. What is actual meaning of it when one says that politics shapes the judicial behavior. Till date, there is no one clear answer to the above question. In the United States, the term does not denote any single phenomenon.

According to some, indeterminacy of law, judiciary's preference for the short-term policies, political related to elections, constitutional ideologies, etc. All these meanings have come into existence either due to history and interpretations or due to courts response to more immediate, external political pressure.

However, it is important to distinguish between the two meanings. Based purely on observation or experience, the different types of political influence vary. Substantial evidence, in some cases, proves that the influence of politics in judicial decision making exist in a great deal while is some, there is absence of such evidences; and there are few such cases as well where claims are essential unfalsifiable.

Hence, it all depends on what politics one is referring to before concluding the influence of politics in judicial decisions. In America, more often the questions related to judicial politics are mixed with questions about the role of courts.

4.3.1. A Taxonomy of "Politics" in Judicial Decision Making

There is a general understanding amongst the students of American courts where they believe that broadly defined 'politics' does influence the judicial decision making. However, this general agreement amongst the students cover different theories, outlook, interpretation of how politics and to what extent it influences the judicial Behavior or decision making.

This means what kind of political influences impacts the courts and what system makes it impact the decision making. The term 'politics as used by scholars describes a wide variety of phenomena. Each phenomenon works on different systematic levels, right from the judge's individual choice in some cases to encompassing the judiciary's role in the government of America.

As such, the meaning seems ok and unobjectionable. In actual, the definition of the term "politics" is quite extensive. Politics is defined as "who gets what, when, [and] how," by Harold Lasswell, whereas David Easton described politics as "the authoritative allocation of values for a society."

In nutshell, the term politics is understood as the fight over the views and values. When the resources are scarce, whose views and values will decide its allocation, who will receive the social advantages and who is going to bear the expenses.

However, different understandings of the term politics have different implications in judicial decision making. Thus, so far there is no clear meaning or definition of politics and its implications on judicial decision making.

4.3.2. Politics as Judicial Discretion

Broadly, if one understands politics as it applies to courts is another name for judicial judgment. If the decisions taken by the judiciary are not according to the accepted legal authority, for example-the appropriate text, history, tradition for example, the judicial decisions are regarded as political.

For example, when a judge gives personal judgment which is outside the realm of law, then the decision made is definitely political. As per Richard Posner, the Supreme Court, when it is deciding constitutional cases, is political in the sense of having and exercising discretionary power as capacious as a legislature.

As a matter of fact, it is obvious that judges enjoy important discretion while taking decisions. As is the nature of the law, it is not in the hands of law to provide objectively correct answers to many legal disputes. Thus, it gives judges the freedom and space to function.

Judges too, being humans, get affected by the cognitive behavioral frame and instincts while exercising this discretion. Though their discretion is not free from boundaries and the level of discretion varies from circumstance to circumstance.

The judges of the Supreme Court experience more freedom and get more open space compared appellate court's judges. What are more important are the factors that shape the way the judges exercise their discretionary power. There is no doubt that the judges in America exercise significant decision in giving their decision (Figure 4.4).

Figure 4.4: Judiciary has a major role to play in eliminating the crimes from the political setup.

Source: Image by Pixabay.

Even after all of this, the concept of politics seems to be too broad to make understanding of judicial behavior in significant ways. Since the authoritative sources of law is often uncertain and vague in most of the cases, at least within a range of reasonable outcomes, people have accepted the idea of discretionary judgment and hence judges in the court takes decision discretionary quite often. In fact, in day to day court's cases, it comes to notice how two judges of equal training, intelligence, and commitments reach opposite conclusions in the same case, while maintaining the rule of law. The point to ponder here is not whether judges exercise discretion or not but how do, they use this discretionary power.

4.4. JUDICIARY: FUNCTIONS, IMPORTANCE, AND AN ESSENTIAL QUALITY OF JUDICIARY

The administration of justice, the judiciary is often called the third organ of the government. It is the duty of the judiciary to give justice to people and settle all disagreements or disputes. The actual 'meaning of law' is the judgment passed by the judges during the course.

In fact, from the citizen's point of view judiciary remains the significant part of the government because judiciary protects the citizens against the legislative and executive bodies. Since Judiciary acts as the guardian-protector of the constitution and fundamental rights of the people, it is more respectable than legislative and executive organs.

4.4.1. Functions of Judiciary and Its Importance

1. **To Provide Justice to the People:** Whenever any individual, group, or entity knocks the door of judiciary, it is the most important duty of the judiciary to provide justice to them. After hearing both the parties, court passes the order to punish to the one found guilty or violating the laws of the state or the fundamental rights of the people.

It is the right of aggrieved citizens to seek redress and compensation. If the aggrieved fear any harm to their rights or have suffered any losses, he/she can opt for redressal and compensation. It is the judiciary who decides on the type and duration of punishment to be given to the culprit. Decision on cases that involves grant of compensations to the citizens is also decided by the judiciary.

2. **Interpretation and Application of Laws:** Apart from giving justice to the people, judiciary has another important role which is to interpret and apply the law to specific cases. Courts interpret and apply the laws to the facts presented during trial, determine what testimony and proof is applicable and then passes the judgment. It is the duty of the judge to make sure that the law is

properly interpreted before applying to every specific case.

3. **Role in Law-Making:** When the judge passes the judgment, that judgment, in fact, determines the meaning, nature, and scope of the laws passed by the legislature. Judiciary's role in interpretation of the law is the success of lawmaking as the meaning, nature, and scope of the law is defined in the interpretations.

Not only that, decisions taken by the higher courts (i.e., courts of records) is to be abided by the lower courts. The lower courts can then decide their specific cases basis the judgment passed by the higher courts. Judicial decisions are regarded as the source of law.

4. **Equity Legislation:** Sometimes, court faces issues where law is silent of ambiguous, or inconsistent with some other law of the land for example, meanings of the words in an agreement are not clear, or is uncertain or leads to various interpretations by different individuals.

In such cases, it is expected that the judge will take decision based on their sense of justice, fairness, unbiased, honesty, and wisdom. The decision involves law-making and is termed as equity legislation.

5. **Protection of Rights:** Citizens of a country are given many rights by the state through the laws of the State. It is the duty of the judiciary to protect these rights. In case, citizens feel that their rights are violated or feel the threat to be violated by any government or private agencies or even by fellow citizens, they have the right to approach to the judiciary to seek protection. It then becomes the responsibility of the judiciary to safeguard the rights of its citizen.
6. **Guardian of the Constitution:** Courts are also called the guardians of the constitution. It is the duty of the judiciary to interpret and protect the constitution which is the supreme law of the land. The judiciary has also the authority to have the judicial review over any law in order to make sure that it is an agreement of the letter of law and a spirit of law, i.e., they are not in conflict.

In the process, if court finds any law which is unconstitutional, under the power of judicial review, judiciary has the right to reject the law and the same becomes invalid for all future cases.

7. **Power to get its Decisions and Judgments Enforced:** The Judicial branch of the government has all the powers to enforce laws. Apart from settling the disputes and delivering the judg-

ment, judiciary has the power to get the same enforced. It can give orders to the executive to adhere to the decision or judgment. The court has the power to summon any individual and question him/her.

If the situation arises, where the individual is held:

i. Guilty of not adhering court's decision;
ii. Going against the court's decision;
iii. Misleading the judiciary;
iv. Of deliberately absenting from the hearing.

Or similar situations, individual can be punished by the court for the contempt of court.

8. **Special Role in a Federation:** Judiciary plays a significant role in the federal system. It acts as the guardian or protector of the constitution and the ultimate authority in case any dispute arises between the center and state. It is the duty of the court to act as an independent and impartial arbiter between the two governments, namely central and state. Judiciary also settles all legal center-state disputes.
9. **Running of the Judicial Administration:** The judiciary is independent of both the legislature and the executive. In fact, each branch, judicial, legislature, and executive are independent from each other. The judiciary is not a department of the government.

Judiciary has its own organization and officials and has the power to decide the nature of judicial organization in the state. Judiciary supervises and takes care of enrolling and working of the magistrates and others working in the courts. It interprets and enforces rules for the fair and efficient conduct of the administration.

10. **Advisory Functions:** Sometimes, the judiciary or the court is authorized to give opinion or advisory views to leaders, such as the President of the country or a Governor of a State. This role by court is played particularly when the matter is of public importance.
11. **To Conduct Judicial Inquiries:** Sometimes, judges head the Enquiry Commissions to investigate the case constituting serious matter which may have arisen due to the alleged errors or omissions by the government or some public servants. Even some important and complicated cases are also handled by the judge heading the Enquiry Commissions.

12. **Miscellaneous Functions:** The functions of the judiciary are not only limited to the ones listed above. There are many other functions of the judiciary.

Some of them are: recruitment of local officials of the court, clerical, and other employees of the court, handles cases related to grant of licenses, patents, and copyrights, guardians, and trustees are appointed by them, admission of wills, the appointment of the trustees to take care of minor's property, to settles disputes arising out of successions of property and rights, issue of administrating the estates of deceased persons, the appointment of receivers, naturalization of aliens, marriage, and divorce cases, election petitions and the like.

Judiciary is an important branch of the government and plays a significant role through all these functions. Judiciary has a part to play in the evolution of Constitution as well where it protects the constitution against all legislative and executive excesses.

4.4.2. Importance of Independent Judiciary

Citizens look upon the Judiciary with confidence and no fear, as their guardian and protector. It is the judiciary who provide justice to the common man. It is difficult for a common man to live a happy, carefree life and do their work without any fear, had there been no security of their rights and freedom.

Citizens of a country depend more on judiciary than on the legislative and executive. This is one of the main reasons as why Judiciary is considered as the significant branch of any government. Life without judicial protection is difficult for the citizens.

According to Garner, "a society without legislature is conceivable, and indeed, legislative organs did not make their appearance in the state until modern times, but a civilized state without a judicial organ and machinery is hardly conceivable."

Judiciary holds its importance because it acts as:

- Justice providers;
- Guardian of people's rights;
- Protector of the constitution of the state;
- Adjudicator of any center-state conflict;
- Safeguard against legislative and executive excesses;

- Check against arbitrary exercise of powers by the power-holders;
- Protector of rule of law and order.

Every democratic government will have an independent judiciary to look after its people. In a democratic government, one can't imagine a government without its important organ, i.e., judiciary. An authoritarian government makes a government without an independent judiciary.

4.5. INDEPENDENCE OF JUDICIARY: AN ESSENTIAL QUALITY

One of the most important factors contributing in favor of judiciary to work honestly and administer justice all the time is its independence. When there is no legislative or executive influence or power imposed upon the judiciary, the judiciary is able to carry out its responsibilities smoothly and independently.

According to Dr. P. Sharan, the independence of judiciary is, "a corner stone of every democratic government and upon it is built the structure of civil liberty." When judiciary is free to dispense justice as per law, it is able to function well. If judiciary is not well organized or is not independent, the purpose of its existence fails. Judiciary should be organized in a manner that gives the judges the power to make decisions fearlessly and impartially.

Organization of Judiciary must be based on the following features:

- Only highly qualified and experienced judges should be on board.
- Safeguarding the judiciary from any executive and legislative excesses.
- Judiciary should be able to control and independently run the judicial administration.
- Judiciary should be the protector of the constitution.
- Just and cost-effective opportunities to be provided by the judiciary to common man to protect their rights and get justice.
- Judges to be appointed through fair, systematic, effective, and transparent means.
- It should not be a cake walk to remove the judges; especially no individual should have the power to remove any judge.
- Judges should be provided with good salaries, necessary

allowances, high service conditions, and appropriate retirement benefits.

A judicial system incorporating all of the above features marks the formation of a well-organized and independent judiciary.

4.6. ROLE OF THE JUDICIARY IN DEMOCRACY

The role of judiciary is quite crucial in a democratic environment. Known as a faithful keeper of the constitution, the judiciary has four significant responsibilities, namely, to formulate the law through the interpretation and application of law, adjudicating a dispute, check legal matters and also act as a kcy playcr in statc politics.

In order to fulfill the above duties and responsibilities, it is important to abide by the basic principles of a liberal democratic state and legal democracy and state.

Not only that, the interpretation and application of the law has to be along with the constitution, along with the unbiased judgment in case of any disputes that arise between the State and individual, between individuals and between different levels of government within the State.

The late twentieth century and early twenty first century saw the rise in the judiciary and people's reliance on the courts and judicial power to address issues related to moral dilemmas, political conflicts and questions related to public policies.

The high court's of the nations around the world are handling various issues right from the right to express to religious liberties, reproductive, and privacy freedoms, right to equality, public policies related to criminal justice, education, labor, and environmental protection.

The growing political importance of courts has become more globally widespread and has lengthened its scope to become a diversified and varied phenomenon that expands beyond the well-known phenomenon of judges making policies.

The Irish Free State (1922) was replaced by the basic law of the Irish State as the constitution of Ireland through referendum in 1937. The constitution of the country is the supreme law of the country. It is an umbrella under which justice is administered and legal rights enforced in the courts.

It is the constitution that describes the powers vested among the legislative, executive, and judiciary where legislative organ makes law, the executive enforces the law, and the judiciary interprets the law. Thus, it takes care of the judicial protection of the fundamental rights of the people. Individuals may invoke to challenge the constitutional laws passed by the Parliament and may plead in case of breach of constitutional rights. The legal system is based on the common law.

The role of the judiciary is exhibited not only in the way what the judges do but how they perform their duty, which is also known as judicial style. However, the judicial style is different for civil law and the common law.

The common man demands and expects the accountability from all the government agencies, which needs to be in sync with the principles of independence. It is the tax money, i.e., the money of common man that is invested in the courts and people expect the courts to function efficiently, including judges to be fair, just, and unbiased, prompt adjudication and manage cases keeping the economy of the country in mind.

The democratic countries have relied on 'the culture of the judiciary.' The first thing when judges are appointed and take charge of the office, they are required to swear to stand by the rights of all citizens and the constitution as a whole, self-integrity, peer pressure, and public scrutiny combine to make judges.

The idea to set these standards for promotion is that they further help their future peers and lower levels to adopt the similar behavior. The duty of just and honor and the principles of natural justice have been established by the courts through judicial review to focus on the essential point whether, under all situations, the procedure followed in a particular case was fair or not.

The clarity and open process of decision-making that have been structured through judicial review acts as one of the protections to achieve an acceptable balance between the country's need for security and the rights and freedoms of its citizens.

To deal with this matter, an intricate approach is required. Judges will continue to depend upon the viewpoints, understanding, wisdom, and knowledge of the legal community. However, in order for judiciary to achieve complete understanding, respective contributions from different disciplines such as community and government employees, academicians, social scientists, and policymakers will be equally important.

As per the new legislation, for the growth and development of logical, sensible, and sound principles, a detailed and complex balance is required.

However, the fact that legislature also has to make sure that it does not force or impact the court's working neither should get involved in the appointment and selection of the court's personnel since it is a party to many conflicts between citizens and their representatives that the court has to put right.

For example, legislature has to admit that their aim is to represent citizens and operate within the boundaries as prescribed in the constitution. However, it is also true that the representation does not means that it remains undisputed power.

It is one of the main functions of the judiciary to safeguard the rights of the citizens even if their duly elected legislative representative actions are against the constitutional rights or outside the boundary of the law as defined in the constitution.

The other branches of government should limit their involvement in the workings of the court in order to function smoothly. In case any rule is found unsuitable, constitution describes the process to make amendments in the constitution itself.

The role of judiciary in formulating or applying the policies is a matter which goes beyond the judicial review of administrative decisions. Formation of policies to be one of the functions of judiciary requires a detailed understanding as what the policy is going to be about and how the same is related to judicial matters.

Also, what will be the role of the judiciary and the scope of judiciary in this policy formation. In response to the changing needs and increasing demand for the justification, quite a development is seen in the common law, where the judges seem to be more accountable for their actions, i.e., the proposed changes and follow the realm of laws as defined in the constitution.

Another matter which is worth considering is the change in the attitude of people towards legal profession where the use of litigation is seen as a way to achieve political and social objectives.

Since long, litigation has been used as a weapon when it comes to corporate and commercial disputes; however, there is an increase in the use of litigation to achieve political and social objectives. As a result, there is a change in the nature of the work that comes before some courts, and has a significant impact in the way in which courts appear to the public to behave.

The country has seen consequential changes in the relationship between its citizens and the nation being a democratic society. Judiciary, being one of the most important organs of the Government, holds great knowledge and experience to make huge contributions to the maintenance and development of the democratic society.

In order to achieve this, it is important that the courts remain completely independent in authority and function from all other participants in the justice system and they continue to resolve disputes, interpret the law, and safeguard the constitution.

4.7. JUDICIAL ETHICS AND THE POLITICAL ROLE OF THE COURTS

That sense of uneasiness and discomfort that Americans felt during the last part of 1960's was very much present as they entered 1970's in a much deeper way. The reason of this uneasiness and discomfort was evident in American's Behavior towards their country, the problems that existed and future prospects.

This Behavior of the people of America alone constitutes a bigger problem especially because of the lack of confidence in every institution of America, especially the political and government agencies. But the problem is much bigger than the just the doubts or lack of confidence in the efficiency of these public institutions.

The much bigger problem is the inclination of people to find an escape from their lack of confidence through efforts to find simple explanations for the problems of the system or to select one from a group or agency that can be blamed for all the troubles. Even people who are unbiased and not influenced by personal prejudices find a little reason to feel positive.

What academicians and learned people argue is that the system as a whole is inadequate to handle its problem. Many people do agree that as in the present scenario, political, and government agencies and their processes lack the ability to handle the task that comes their way.

The resulting crisis is easily the most severe the nation has faced since the Great Depression of the 1930s. In many aspects, the problem is far more serious, since the issues are more emotionally charged, the sources of the problem are spread out over a wide area, and problem, of course, does not seem to be managed on its own.

Even the courts are still in that doubt zone affecting our political institutions. Public are highly dissatisfied with the judiciary adjudication, especially those passed by the United States Supreme Court which has resulted in the level of confidence in the courts and the judicial process. When the people involved in judicial proceedings exhibit their disregard for the judiciary and they refuse to follow the standards of appropriate behavior that have before the time is assumed to be the condition of the judicial process, the disappointment with the court is even fierce.

Chief Justice Warren E Burger on an overwhelming proportion of the bench, bar, and public, demanded for the new rules of courtroom behavior that would "eliminate some of the spectacles that are undermining public confidence in the whole [judicial] system."

Many recent court proceedings in America demonstrated this aspect of the problem; however, the trial of Chicago Seven in 1969 and 1970 is the perfect example of the said problem. This trial was originally billed as a test of the 1968 Civil Rights Act provision.

It was a federal violation if any individuals cross the state lines with the intentions to provoke a riot. For many different reasons, the said trial became a landmark in the history of judicial proceedings and clearly pointed out the breakable, delicate nature of the judicial process and conveying very clearly how sensitive that process is to the disturbing behavior of those who disregard the rules of procedure and etiquette normally expected in American courts of law.

It was evident from the beginning of this trial, that the defendants have made up their mind to test the limits of judicial tolerance. Their unruly behavior, jokes related to judge and lack of respect for the courtroom rules didn't even meet the basics of the judicial process:

They were all motivated by the belief that they were part of an act that is an insult to the system of justice. Defendant's and their legal representatives' questionable and doubtful behavior was matched by many aspects by the behavior of the trial judge's.

However, the judge tried to hide his disrespect for both the defendants and their attorneys. Finally, one of the defendants was ordered to stay silence after repetitive disturbance and harassment while the trial proceeded.

This along with many such dramatic and disrespect actions by the trial judge led many people to conclude that his conduct was unquestionably biased against the defense. The famous Chicago Seven trial blatantly reveals the basic flaw in the judicial process, especially the limitations to deal with those who have the courage to carry disrespect and discourtesy into the courtroom.

What should be the way out when the defendants who very openly disrespect the judge, the court and the law either through disregardful words or actions or through failure to comply with the court's code of conduct?

What can people expect if for such disrespectful behavior, the judge in return is kind and makes no effort to counter this disrespectful behavior or doesn't stand for the values? According to Chief Justice Burger, some method must be found for removing such issues from the judicial proceedings.

However, simple changes in court procedures are not sufficient to solve the problem nor the rebuilding of courtroom decorum will help to revive the long-lost public confidence in the courts. Because all these problems lack depth and are more casual and serves as a symptom only of basic factors that have actually eaten away at the foundations of the judicial process.

Certainly, the militant, "anti-establishment" political element in our society will not have its faith in the courts restored by procedural reforms. Recent Supreme Court's decision on cases involving racial segregation and civil rights has won the confidence and faith of many political dissidents in the judiciary branch of the Government compared to any other branch of the government.

The court's action in restricting disorders, protests, and demonstrations, in the courtroom as well as the cities eventually led most political dissents to believe that the judiciary could not be trusted either as it is just another agency to control the riot and control the political dissents. The courts are thus caught in a damaging cross-fire.

Political militants are the ones who are in need of the protection the most by the judiciary, contempt the procedures that is the basic element of the judicial process. The reason they do so is because they feel that the procedures themselves often lack the impartiality claimed for them, serving instead to favor litigants who identify with the status quo.

Political activist also holds the view that the judges are partial against them since the beginning. Though they are not wrong but they make a mistake when they change these beliefs or observations into the plan that all the courtroom's practices intended to be impartial and unbiased and not influenced by personal prejudices of the bench, is all pretense intended to obscure the truth that the legal 'game' is fixed so that they can never win.

It is seen that any interruption of courtroom trial by political dissents, whether blacks or leftists, millions of other Americans cringe in disgust. In particular, the political conservatives, a lot of importance on bringing back the honor of the judicial process. According to them respect for the representative of law and order, the police force and the judges, is the base of societal order.

When these conservatives cry over the dishonor shown towards the legal institutions, they forget that not long ago when they were passing the nasty comments, secretly agreeing with "impeach Earl Warren" slogan and were openly campaigning disrespect to court orders.

Amongst these were also the esteemed groups such as the Conference of State Chief Justices and the American Bar Association who attacked the Supreme Court, publicly criticizing the court and charging it with having exceeded its legitimate powers and role.

It is no wonder that young political activists readily move toward displays of dishonesty for the judicial institutions. What is done by the most respected groups in society is simply followed by these young activists.

However, they have their own over-dramatic way of complaining political style. Still, the problems surrounding our courts are not going to subside, even if the leftist-oriented and black political militants suddenly decide to go away from the American political scene.

Because the problems that have surrounded the judicial system is not going to go easily till the time the problems have political connection, the judicial institutions will find themselves surrounded by politically troubled issues.

However, if people want to see and expect a different outcome, it requires many big assumptions including the fundamentally different role of the courts than present in the American system.

To expect any refrain of politics, the very unlikely assumption is to be made like the assumption that there is a complete transformation of governmental political system in a way that the executive and legislative branches of the government are able to handle the system's problems on their own. Justification for these conclusions needs further elaboration upon three propositions:

- The affirmation that current political controversy surrounding the judiciary is the result of the types of political issues that currently rule the political life;
- The idea that these issues come to be forced upon the courts, in part, because of the particular role of the courts (particularly the supreme court) in one's political life; and

- As a conclusion of this second proposition, the contention that the courts assume such a role largely because of the failure of other branches of the government.

These arguments will be dealt with in the following section, to be followed by a third section examining the result that these features of the judiciary's role have for issues relating to judicial ethics.

What is implicit in this order of presentation is the premise that questions relating to norms of judicial conduct cannot be answered until one understands the role of the judiciary in the political-governmental system, the nature of the demands made upon the judiciary, and the sources of support that it has.

4.8. EFFECTIVENESS AND FAIRNESS OF JUDICIAL SYSTEMS

It is a right of the citizens of the country to expect the decisions of the court to be effective and fair. The civil justice system, if functioning fairly and effectively, acts as the guardian and safeguards the rights of the citizens against any breach of the law, including any powerful parties and government.

In fact, one of the main components of the rule of law is an effective and just judicial system. This way it validates that, the laws are respected and necessary measures are taken when the laws are broken.

However, it is not easy to keep the well-functioning judiciary system away from the other stakeholders like police and the correctional systems especially when it comes to cases involving security and crime.

4.8.1. Effectiveness and Independence in the Implementation of Civil Justice Decisions

There is a need of detailed rules, regulations, and steps to make sure the independence of civil justice while adjudicating any dispute in an impartial way.

As per the data collected from the World Justice Report, there is a strong connection between people's understanding that civil justice is capably and efficiently implemented and their understanding that the civil justice is not concerned or bothered by any external factors like improper government influence, etc.

As a matter of fact, in countries like Norway, the Netherlands, Sweden, Austria, Germany, Denmark, Finland, and Australia, their citizens and justice experts claims that their judicial system was effective in enforcing laws and their government's interference was minimal in the civil justice system.

4.8.2. Effectiveness of Criminal Justice Systems and Citizens' Protection Against Crime

Just like civil justice system, an efficient and fair criminal justice system is also competent enough to investigate and adjudicate criminal cases in the most effective and unbiased manner, keeping in mind that the rights of both the suspect and victim is safeguarded.

However, the evaluation of the criminal justice system should take into consideration the complete system like police, lawyers, prosecutors, judges, and prison officers (Botero and Ponce, 2012). As per the 2014 data from the World Justice Report, people of those countries which perceived the criminal justice system as timely, efficient, and just reported the lower inclination to resort to violence to compensate for the personal grievances for example, riot violence against government.

The relatively high correlation (R2 = 0.9) between those two sub-dimensions of the WJP Rule of Law Index suggest that the effective, timely, and just criminal justice system is a key to maintain security and societal solidarity at the country level.

As per 2014 data, in almost all OECD countries, the crime was efficiently controlled and was high in number as compared to other major countries, Mexico being the exception. However, this data pertains to only three major urban areas in each of the OECD countries mentioned above and is based on the perception and understanding of the people.

It may also be the case that when data was collected, some sensitive cases had just been handled. Moreover, more work is required to be done in the years to come to establish more clearly the connection between the efficient judicial systems and their influence in the fairness, law, and order in OECD and other nations.

4.9. THE STRUCTURE OF CRIMINAL JUSTICE

Criminal justice, as a term, includes federal, state, and local public agencies who handle the cases related to crime. These judiciaries are independent of each other and take decisions involving suspects, defendants, and convicted offenders and as such, the decision taken by one agency does not affect the other agencies. However, the basic structure of the system is provided by the legislative, executive, and judicial part of the government (Figure 4.5).

Figure 4.5: The judicial systems work to provide criminal justice.

Source: Image by Pixabay.

- **The Legislature:** Both state and federal legislature define crimes, fix sentences, and funding for criminal justice agencies are also looked after them.
- **The Judiciary:** Trial courts adjudicate the disputes and makes decision against the person guilty of the crime, whereas appellate courts interpret the law as per the constitutional principles. The legislative decisions are reviewed by the state and federal appellate courts and they decide whether they have crossed the boundaries of any state, federal or the constitution as such, or not.

The courts are given the power by the judicial review to evaluate legislative acts to see if they fall within the boundaries of the constitution. If the appellate court finds that the law is in conflict with the constitution, the said law may strike it down and make it invalid.

- **The Executive Branch:** The president, governors, and mayors are conferred the executive powers, where they have the power to appoint judges and heads of agencies in criminal justice cases, such as police chiefs and directors of correction departments. Moreover, the elected personnel can take charge to put forward the legislative agendas and mobilize public opinion in order to improve criminal justice (Figure 4.6).

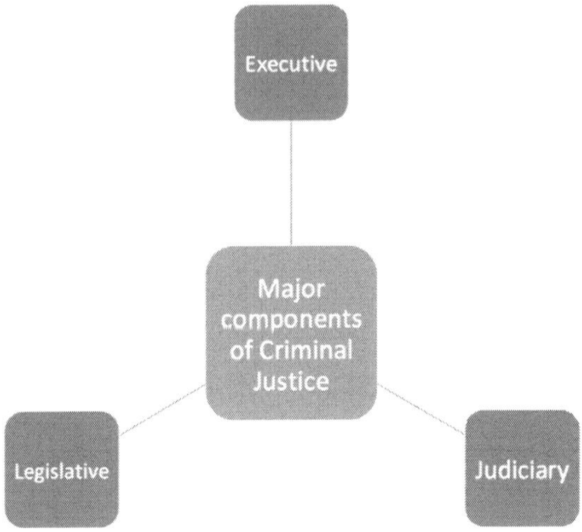

Figure 4.6: Major components of the criminal justice system.

4.9.1. The Major Components of the Justice System

The way justice system, i.e., courts, police, and correction department as a whole work to prevent crime is by arresting and punishing the culprit. It is the function of the police department to maintain law and order in the city/ state, administer the criminal law, and provide services to the citizens.

Their job is to deter and control crime in the community. Moreover, they also work hand in hand with the prosecutors and help in investigation criminal cases, gathering proofs against the culprit in order to obtain convictions in the court.

Courts are tribunals where the accused come to get their criminal responsibility decided by the judges. It is the first and foremost aim of the court to give justice and to find out the truth. Judges, prosecutors, and defense attorneys are the key players in the court.

Punishment varies and includes probation, imprisonment, parole, and many different new community-based sanctions such as electronic monitoring and even house arrest. The correctional agencies aim is to punish, to rehabilitate, and to safeguard public safety.

4.9.2. The Differences Between Federal and State Justice Systems

No doubt, the functions carried by the federal and state justice systems are same such as law enforcement, trial cases, passing judgments and punishing the lawbreakers, yet they are different. The laws and agencies of the two systems are different. State jurisdiction is broad and handles cases such as robberies, broken contracts, traffic violations.

Criminal cases involving violation of State law are also handling in State Court. At the federal level, criminal laws are executed by the Congress and federal law enforcement agencies, such as the Federal Bureau of Investigation, enforce these laws.

U.S. attorneys bring action against the persons accused of committing federal crimes and U.S. courts try the cases. To punish and rehabilitate those find guilty of federal crimes, the Federal Bureau of Prisons provides programs and institutions.

4.9.3. The First Line of Defense Against Crime

In the United States, the administration of justice is looked after by a State or Local Government. As a result, two-thirds of all criminal justice workers are employed by the State and local government.

Federal Government pays much less share of the costs of criminal justice compared to State and Local government. This is because the state, county, and city criminal justice agencies are the ones who provide the citizens protection from the thieves, rapists, and murderers.

4.9.4. Criminal Justice as a Non-System

Critics characterize criminal justice as a nonsystem. According to the critics, the criminal justice agencies are independent and their power, authority, and budgets are all from varied sources. Such as, towns, and cities funds for the police department whereas country (as a whole) funds for the prosecutors, public defenders, trial courts, and jails.

Whereas State usually funds for the prisons and appellate courts. Moreover, criminal justice agencies publish their own policies. It gets also difficult for the criminal justice agencies to coordinate their and as a result they often tend to ignore the consequences their decisions will have on other agencies.

4.10. CONCLUSION

Judiciary holds a great deal of significance in the political system of a state. The various laws, legal tenders, regulations, bills, and acts are checked by the Judiciary and it is responsibility of the judiciary to ensure that these laws and regulations are followed by the people and that the victims can get justice in any kind of crime.

The judiciary also ensures that there is no tampering with the political systems in form of any criminal activity. The judiciary is expected to be fair and also extremely effective in terms of implementing the laws. It assumes more important role in a democracy and hence must be independent of any other body, so that justice can be ensured.

REFERENCES

1. Cliffsnotes.com. (n.d.). *The Structure of Criminal Justice.* [online] Available at: https://www.cliffsnotes.com/study-guides/criminal-justice/the-criminal-justice-system/the-structure-of-criminal-justice (accessed on 25 April 2020).
2. Downing, R., (2020). *Judicial Ethics and the Political Role of the Courts*. [eBook] Available at: https://scholarship.law.duke.edu/cgi/viewcontent.cgi?article=3278&context=lcp (accessed on 25 April 2020).
3. Encyclopedia Britannica, (n.d.). *Judiciary | Government.* [online] Available at: https://www.britannica.com/topic/judiciary (accessed on 25 April 2020).
4. Ghai, K., (n.d.). *Judiciary: Functions, Importance, and an Essential Quality of Judiciary*. [online] Your Article Library. Available at: http://www.yourarticlelibrary.com/essay/law-essay/judiciary-functions-importance-and-an-essential-quality-of-judiciary/40352 (accessed on 25 April 2020).
5. Government at a Glance, (2015). *Government at a Glance 2015.* [online] Available at: https://www.oecd-ilibrary.org/docserver/gov_glance-2015-en.pdf?expires=1585314280&id=id&accname=guest&checksum=3F862F093DD2798CD4D2541225CE5101 (accessed on 25 April 2020).
6. Joondeph, B., (2008). *The Many Meanings of "Politics" in Judicial Decision Making*. [eBook] Santa Clara University School of Law. Available at: https://digitalcommons.law.scu.edu/cgi/viewcontent.cgi?article=1036&context=facpubs (accessed on 25 April 2020).
7. Lawteacher.net. (2018). *The Concept of Judicial Independence.* [online] Available at: https://www.lawteacher.net/free-law-essays/constitutional-law/the-concept-of-judicial-independence-law-essay.php (accessed on 25 April 2020).
8. UKEssays.com. (2018). *Role of the Judiciary in Democracy*. [online] Available at: https://www.ukessays.com/essays/politics/role-of-judiciary-in-democracy.php (accessed on 25 April 2020).

Chapter 5

Violation of Human Rights: The Role of Politics

CONTENTS

Human rights are the most basic rights that a human must have so as to live peacefully and in an informed way. These rights covert the right to food, water, clean air, education, and no violence. Politics has been historically criticized for being the depriver of human rights to various groups of people as per their liking and suiting, whereas they are in charge to protect and preserve those rights.

This chapter throws light on the various human rights, their importance, the efforts been taken to ensure them, and the way in which these rights are violated at various levels of governance and politics, making it a criminal activity.

5.1. INTRODUCTION

One of the most prevalent features of the current political scenario is the concept of human rights co-existing with the practices and various institutions that give expression to it. In spite of this pervasiveness, the discipline of political science has seen only a marginal occupation within it by the subject of human rights.

The study of human rights cannot be said to belong to the mainstream of political science even though within political science an important theme has been the conceptual analysis if 'rights' and the research done by some scholars has been totally devoted it.

As a result of this marginal position, very few courses of politics are devoted to it even in a partial manner. In 1989, an international survey was undertaken on the human rights courses and it underlined the limited contribution that political science has made to the subject of human rights.

Furthermore, in 1991 an analysis was done in the US to see the place that human rights occupied within the textbooks which found that human rights were not seen by most American political scientists as an important aspect of international relations even though the foreign policy was showing an increasing impact of human rights (Figure 5.1).

Figure 5.1: The human rights govern the way people live their lives.

Source: Image by Pixabay.

The reasons behind this marginal position of human rights are fairly easy to fathom. The skepticism that is has been forever existing with respect to the status that human rights occupy within the branches of political science (like comparative politics, political theory, and international relations) is the most obvious reason for this.

The appropriateness of the rights-standards and concepts as derived from the west may be questioned by the students of comparative politics whereby different levels of economic development and political traditions guide different societies.

The philosophical presuppositions of human rights make political theorists uncomfortable and at the same time the limitations of any human rights projects at the practical level where states control the means of law enforcement that makes it effective and the loyalties being horned by ethnic and national loyalties remains the area of study in international relations.

Political theory has been one source of skepticism with regard to human rights that is the oldest going back to the critical responses of varying degrees that were made to the French revolution's declaration of the rights of man.

As pointed out by Burke and other conservatives the specific legal orders and traditions that are prevalent in a nation and within which the rights have evolved over a period of time in a particular set up are the best means whereby these meaningful rights can be protected (Figure 5.2).

Figure 5.2: Human rights protect the people against any judicial injustice as well.

Source: Image by Pixabay.

According to Bentham and other utilitarian, various illusory and vague rights of man cannot give justification to the rights; it is the principle of utility that gives justification to various positive political rights that can be considered as 'rights.

Various feminists like Wollstonecraft have openly criticized the fact that women have been excluded from the so-called rights of man for vague reasons like not being considered 'human' fully or where the state-oriented definition of human rights that is predominantly male-oriented does not include the specific ways in which the rights of the women are violated by men.

> Human rights are the basic rights and freedoms that belong to every person in the world, from birth until death. They apply regardless of where you are from, what you believe or how you choose to live your life. They can never be taken away, although they can sometimes be restricted – for example if a person breaks the law, or in the interests of national security. These basic rights are based on shared values like dignity, fairness, equality, respect, and Independence.

On the other hand, Marxists believed that the stage of historical evolution that was bourgeois and lower had a predominance of the rights-claim which needs to go beyond these boundaries by way of an all-around development of the capacities of humans and cooperation amongst them that can be brought about in a communist society.

'Foundationalism' (the attempts towards bringing the rights within human rationality or human nature that is universal), has been rejected by the contemporary political philosophy which adds to the various different strands of skepticism that have been existing through history which insists that the most fundamental conceptions are dependent on the context aspect. Thus, the most relevant political aspect is not the asserting of similarities but the negotiation of differences.

5.2. WHAT ARE HUMAN RIGHTS?

Rights that accrue to human beings by the very virtue of their existence irrespective of race, ethnicity, nationality, sex, religion, language or any other status are essentially human rights.

These include the freedom of opinion and expression, freedom from slavery and torture, the right to life and liberty, the right to work and education and numerous other rights. Without any discrimination, all are entitled to these rights.

5.2.1. International Human Rights Law

The Government of a State is obliged to act or refrain from acting in specific ways vide the parameters laid out in the international human rights law so that the fundamental freedom of individuals and groups as well as their human rights can be both protected and promoted. The creation of a human rights law that is comprehensive is perhaps one of the greatest achievements of the United Nations which is an internationally protected universal code that can be subscribed by all individuals and aspired to by all people.

A broad range of rights that are accepted internationally have been defined by the United Nations and these include various civil, economic, cultural, social, and political rights. Mechanisms have also been established to protect and promote these rights whereby states are assisted whilst they carry out their responsibilities in this aspect.

The Charter of the United Nations adopted in 1945 and the Universal Declaration of Human Rights (UDHR) which was adopted in 1948 laid the foundations of this body of law.

The human rights law has thereafter been gradually expanded by the United Nations whereby it now encompasses the specific standards which are relevant to children, women, persons with disabilities, vulnerable groups and various minorities giving them various rights and protecting them from the discrimination that has been prevalent in the societies for long.

5.2.2. United Nations

Almost every country across the globe is a member of the United Nations making it a global organization. Various human rights bodies are the key to the promotion of human rights protection and promotion by the United Nations.

5.2.2.1 Human Rights Council

The Human Rights Council has the responsibility for promoting and protecting human rights as well as the strengthening thereof across the world as entailed in the UN Charter which called upon the creation of such an inter-governmental body.

Forty-seven UN member countries comprise the Human Rights Council who conduct a Universal Periodic Review of human rights through regular meetings, addressing the situations across the world where human rights are being violated and at the same time, they receive complaints as well as make recommendations with respect to the manner in which the fulfillment of human rights can be improved.

Independent experts are able to hold mandates to monitor, examine, advise, and report publicly on a thematic human rights issue or the situation of human rights with respect to a specific country though the Special Procedures of the Human Rights Council.

5.2.2.2. Treaty Monitoring Bodies

International human rights treaties that are at the core are nine. In order to monitor the implementation of the treaty provisions by the countries that have ratified the treaty, a committee of experts has been established by each treaty.

In certain cases, some treaties permit them to receive complaints where there has been a violation of human rights of individuals and others. The nine core human rights treaties along with their adoption years are given in Table 5.1.

Table 5.1: Nine Core Human Rights Treaties

Treaty	**Acronym**	**Year**
International convention on the elimination of all forms of racial discrimination	CERD	1965
International covenant on civil and political rights	ICCPR	1966
International covenant on economic, social and cultural rights	ICESCR	1966
Convention on the elimination of all forms of discrimination against women	CEDAW	1979
Convention against torture and other cruel, inhuman or degrading treatment or punishment	CAT	1984
Convention on the rights of the child	CRC	1989
International convention on the protection of the rights of all migrant workers and members of their families	CRMW	1990
Convention on the rights of persons with disabilities	CRPD	2006
International convention for the protection of all persons from enforced disappearance	CED	2006

Source: https://www.theadvocatesforhumanrights.org/uploads/ch_2_2.pdf.

5.2.2.3. Office of the High Commissioner for Human Rights (OHCHR) and Other UN Agencies

United Nations center of most human rights activities is the OHCHR. UN actions to promote and protect human rights are coordinated by it and it ensures the education as well as the implementation of human rights standards through various regional as well as country offices that work with the local partners. The work of the core treaty monitoring bodies and that of the Human Rights Council is supported by the OHCHR. Various other agencies within the UN like the UN High Commissioner for Refugees and the UN Development Program deal with issues related to human rights.

By drafting non-binding international standards whereby international consensus on human rights issues is reflected like the principles, declarations, and guidelines, the United Nations helps to expand the understanding of the world with respect to the content and scope of human rights. Certain examples of these instruments are:

- Declaration on the human rights of individuals who are not nationals of the country in which they live;
- Declaration on the rights of persons belonging to national or ethnic, religious, and linguistic minorities;
- Standard minimum rules for the treatment of prisoners;
- Principles for the protection of all persons under any form of detention or imprisonment;
- Declaration on the rights of indigenous peoples;
- Indigenous and tribal peoples convention.

5.2.3. Other International Human Rights Bodies

Many international organizations other than the United Nations too are involved in the creation, enforcing, and monitoring of the standards of international human rights. Specific categories of human rights issues are focused upon by these international organizations whereas the geographic region forms the area of focus for the others.

Human rights related to work are guaranteed through various legally binding conventions overseen by the International Labor Organization (ILO) specifically the freedom of association and the effective recognition of the right to collective bargaining, the elimination of discrimination when it comes to occupation and employment and the elimination of all forms of compulsory or forced labor.

Individuals who have been accused of the most serious international crimes like crimes against humanity, genocide, and war crimes are tried by an independent court the International Criminal Court (ICC) which is a permanent body.

The Rome Statute which is a treaty ratified by 122 countries complements the national legal system and provides the jurisdiction over these crimes forming forms the basis of the ICC.

5.3. UNIVERSAL DECLARATION OF HUMAN RIGHTS (UDHR)

A milestone document in the history of the human rights is the UDHR. Representatives with varying backgrounds in the cultural and legal fields from across all the regions have drafted the Declaration which was to be a common standard to be achieved by all people across all nations and was proclaimed in Paris on 10 December 1948 by the United Nations General Assembly through the General Assembly resolution 217A(III).

For the first time, the fundamental human rights that are to be protected universally were set out through this Declaration. The UDHR has seen translation into more than five hundred languages since its adoption in 1948 making it to be the document that has been translated the maximum number of times and the constitution of many States that have gained Independence newly has been inspired by this declaration (Figure 5.3).

Figure 5.3: UN general assembly on human rights.

Source: Image by US Department of State.

The international bill of human rights comprises of the UDHR along with the International Covenant on Economic, Social, and Cultural Rights and its Optional protocol and the International Covenant on Civil and

Political Rights and its two optional protocols (on death penalty and the complaints procedure).

- Guiding principles on business and human rights;
- United Nations principles for older persons; and
- United Nations rules for the protection of juveniles deprived of their liberty.

5.3.1. Economic, Social, and Cultural Rights

In 1976, the International Covenant on Economic, Social, and Cultural Rights entered into force. The covenant seeks to protect and promote various human rights that include:

- The right to education and the enjoyment of benefits of scientific progress and cultural freedom.
- The right to an adequate standard of living, social protection and to the highest attainable standards of physical and mental well-being.
- The right to work in conditions that are favorable and just.

5.3.2. Civil and Political Rights

In 1976, the International Covenant on Civil and Political Rights and its First Optional Protocol came into force whereas the adoption of the Second Optional Protocol came about in 1989.

Various rights like the freedom of thought, conscience, and religion; freedom of movement; freedom of association; freedom of opinion and expression; equality before the law; participation in public affairs and elections; the right to a fair trial and presumption of innocence and protection of minority rights are dealt with by the Covenant.

Arbitrary deprivation of life; slavery and forced labor; degrading or cruel treatment, torture or punishment; arbitrary interference with privacy; arbitrary detention or arrest; discrimination; war propaganda and advocacy of religious or racial hatred is prohibited by it (Figure 5.4).

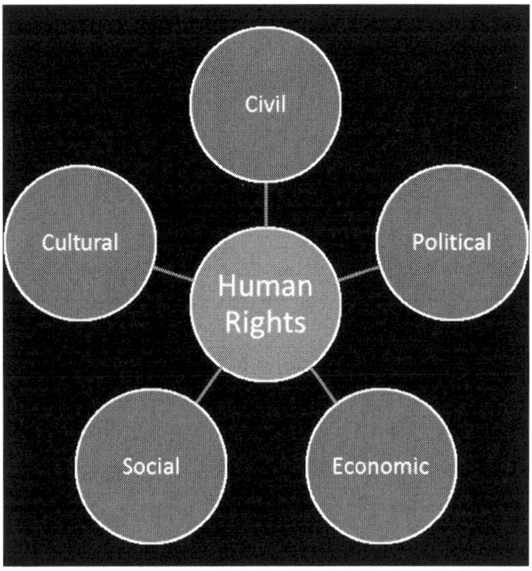

Figure 5.4: Kinds of human rights.

5.4. HUMAN RIGHTS CONVENTIONS

The body of the international human rights law has been expanded since 1945 through the adoption of a number of treaties on international human rights and various other instruments. These include among others:

- The convention on the prevention and punishment of the crime of genocide (1948),
- The International Convention on the elimination of all forms of racial discrimination (1965),
- The convention on the elimination of all forms of discrimination against women (1979),
- The convention on the rights of the child (1989); and
- The convention on the rights of persons with disabilities (2006).

5.4.1. Human Rights Council

The UN Commission on Human Rights which had been existence for sixty years was replaced on 15 March 2006 by the Human Rights Council which was established by the General Assembly to which it reported directly as the key intergovernmental body of the UN that is responsible for human rights.

Forty-seven State representatives comprise the Council which has the important task of protecting and promoting human rights across the globe through the addressing of situations where violations of human rights are taking place and making relevant recommendations thereon which includes response to the emergencies in respect of human rights.

The Universal Periodic Review is the most innovative feature of the Human rights council. Once in every four years, the human rights records of all the 192 UN member states are reviewed through this unique mechanism.

Under the auspices of the Council this review is undertaken in a cooperative manner by the states whereby opportunity is provided to each state to present various challenges they have encountered and met as well as the measures undertaken by them to bring about an improvement in the situation of human rights within their country so that international obligations are met. Equality of treatment and universality for every country is ensured through the design of the Review.

5.4.2. UN High Commissioner for Human Rights

The principle responsibility for the human rights related activities for the UN is exercised by the United Nations High Commissioner for Human Rights. The mandate to undertake preventive action and respond to violations of a serious nature with regard to human rights is vested in the High Commissioner.

The focal point for the human rights activities of the United Nations is the Office of the High Commissioner for Human Rights (OHCHR). The OHCHR serves as the secretariat for the treaty bodies (other than the ones that monitor compliance with the treaties), the Human Rights Council, and the other human rights organs of the United Nations. Field activities with respect to human rights too are undertaken by it.

An oversight body exists for most of the core treaties of human rights which have the responsibility of reviewing the treaty implementation by the countries by which it has been ratified. Complaints can be filed directly to the Committees overseeing the human rights treaties where there has been a violation of the rights of the individuals.

5.4.3. Human Rights and the UN System

Within the key areas of security and peace, humanitarian assistance, development, social, and economic affairs, human rights are a theme that cuts across all the programs and policies of the UN. As a consequence of this, there is an involvement of all the specialized agencies and bodies of the UN in the protection of human rights to some or the other degree.

These include among others the right to food which is advocated by the UN Food and Agriculture organization, the right to development incorporated in the Sustainable Development Goals, gender equality being promulgated by the UN Women, labor rights which have been defined and protected by the ILO, the rights of the disabled people, of the indigenous and the rights of the children. Every year, 10 December is observed as the Human Rights Day.

5.5. THE EXISTENCE AND GROUNDS OF HUMAN RIGHTS

5.5.1. How Can Human Rights Exist?

The manner of existence of these human rights raises a philosophical question for many people. This section explores many ways that possible.

The norms that are created at the international as well as the national level by way of customs, enactments, and decisions that have a judicial genesis is one obvious way to which human rights owe their existence. Treaties turn human rights norms into international law at the international level.

For instance, treaties have given force to the human right not be held in servitude or slavery through Article 8 of the International Covenant on Civil and Political Rights (UN, 1966) and Article 4 of the European Convention for the Protection of Human Rights and Fundamental freedoms (Council of Europe, 1950).

On the other hand, enactments made by the legislature, custom or a judicial decision become a part of the country's law at the national level giving life to the human rights norms. For instance, the 13th Amendment to the U.S. Constitution prohibits servitude and slavery hence providing the right against slavery.

At the national level when the law imbibes human rights it takes the shape of constitutional or civil rights whereas at the international level they are spoken of as human rights.

One of the ways in which human rights exist is via enactments in the law at the international and national level. However, it has been pointed out by many that this is not the only way. Were this to be the case, the availability of human rights would be dependent on the political developments that take place at the international and domestic front.

The idea that the roots of human rights are less subject to and far deeper with respect to human decisions rather than legal enactments has been supported by many people. It has been believed strongly by some that these rights are inherent to humans accruing upon them due to their very fact of existence (Morsink, 2009).

Normative status given to these rights could be seen as inherent due to them having been given by God. The natural rights of pursuit of happiness, life, and liberty are seen to be endowed in humans by the creator as per the U.S. Declaration of Independence (1776). This view thus holds that some basic human rights have been enacted be the supreme lawmaker, God.

Not being restricted to just the current times and having been applied across thousands of years these rights were probably attributed to a decree that was divine in origin so it needed to be abstract (liberty, life, etc.) and very general.

However, the contemporary human rights presuppose contemporary institutions and are far more specific (e.g., right to education and the right to a fair trial). An explanation needs to be given as to how specific rights as found in the treaties and declarations in the contemporary times have been derived from the abstract and general rights even if it is to be believed that these are natural, God-given rights.

Even though at the metaphysical level human rights may seem to have a secure status by attributing their origin to God, at the practical level it does not make them secure in a diverse world. The Godly figure as seen in Islam, Christianity, and Judaism is not agreed to by billions of people.

Where theological beliefs give way to the existence of human rights and their sanctity, these people who do not believe in God or the kind of God who grants such rights, need to be persuaded through a theological view that supports rights.

Persuading them with respect to human rights may not be as tough as convincing them with respect to this view. For all practical purposes, enactment of laws at the international and national level proves to be far more fruitful.

Where human rights are a part of the human moralities at the ground level the existence of human rights becomes possible even without the existence of legal enactments. Specific values (for instance, human life needs to be valued) and specific norms (for instance, intentional murder of an innocent individual is prohibited form a part of these moralities.

If the norm of prohibition of murder is contained in the moralities of all human rights, it would partially make up the right to life which is an essential human right.

It is a rather difficult proposition that the human rights are essentially norms that exist in human moralities of all kinds even though it seems to be an attractive viewpoint. Moral unanimity over the existence of human rights is still missing even though human rights are being widely accepted throughout the world in since the last few decades (Universal Human Rights in a World of Diverse Beliefs and Practices).

Not to get restricted by describing the moral consensus that is in existence, the existing norms are intended to be changed through the treaties and declarations on human rights.

Another way of looking at and describing human rights is to explain them as existing in ethical outlooks that are justified or true. On these lines, if one says that human rights exist against torture it basically connotes that there have always been strong moral grounds that proscribe torture as something wrong and against which protection must be provided.

On the same grounds, attempts towards creation of a political morality that is justified for the entire planet seem to have been made through the Universal Declaration.

It was an attempt to use various practical and moral reasons to support a consensus rather than simply attempting to identify a moral consensus that was already on existence. For these very reasons, an objective commitment towards them is required in this approach.

It goes on the belief that individuals are capable of demanding justifiably from the government as well as from each other and the same can be reliably found out in the same manner as finding out as to how buildings are made durable and sturdy or the working of the physical world per se.

If humans keep an open-mind and get committed towards, serious political and moral inquiry rational agreement is available to them even if currently there is no unanimity about human rights.

Different moral norms than those that are currently enacted or accepted can be generated where the existence of moral reasons is independent of human construction when they are combined with the true facts with respect to current problems, institutions, and resources. This assumption seems to be the grounds for the working of the Universal Declaration (see Morsink, 2009). The main problem with this belief is that existence merely for reasons seems to be a bare existence in the case of human rights.

However, rather than seeing this as a theoretical problem, it can be seen as a practical problem which can be set right by the bringing about by formulation and enacting legal norms. Moral existence that comes into force by virtue of its acceptance on a large scale based on reasons that are both practically and morally strong along with a robust legal existence give the human rights an existence that is best of all.

5.5.2. Normative Justifications for Human Rights

The main features of human rights as well as their character as rights, the high priority they have and their universal application should be defended in their justifications. A starting point should be provided by such justifications so that the plausible list of rights that are specific can be justified (Nickel, 2007 on starting points and making the transition to specific rights, Which Rights are Human Rights).

All the same, additional steps may be required for justifying international human rights (Buchanan, 2012). It thus becomes a daunting task to construct a justification for human rights that is good.

Human rights should be given a strong theoretical basis for its justification through human well-being (Summer, 1987; Talbott, 2010); autonomy and agency (Gewirth, 1996; Griffin, 2008); prudential reasons, moral rights and practical reasons (Thomson, 1990); equality and positive freedom (Nussbaum, 2000; Gould, 2004; Sen, 2004); fairness (Nickel, 2007); dignity (Kateb, 2011; Tasioulas, 2015; Gilabert, 2018); human needs (Miller, 2012) and fundamental interests (Beitz, 2015).

Even though justifications can appeal to several and be eclectic, they can also be based on only one of these different types of reasons (Tasioulas, 2015).

In the recent years, there have been strong advocates for grounding human rights in autonomy and human agency. For instance, an agency-based justification for human rights was offered by Alan Gewith in Human Rights: Essays on Justification and Application (1982).

He strongly advocated that human beings do not have the option of denying the value of action and successful agency; action and the agency are indispensable conditions required for the overall good of a living being and are necessary for life. In abstract terms, well-being and freedom are the conditions of successful agency.

A "prudential right claim" shall be asserted towards them by a prudent rational agent who must have both wellbeing and freedom. If an individual wants the others to respect the well-being or freedom that one possesses, he/she should respect the same with regard to the others as all individuals have the same needs which require the respecting of well-being and freedom?

One must accept and respect the fact that as agents, other people too have equal rights to their well-being and freedom. Equal, specific human rights which are kind of familiar are created by these two abstract rights that work together and alone at times (Gewirth, 1978, 1982, 1996).

Gewrith aspired to cater for an all applicable argument with respect to human rights that is inescapable and applicable to all human agents. Two generic rights have been considered as derivable by him on the basis of the principle of consistency and few facts that are difficult to dispute and further a list of more determinate rights from them. A large critical literature has been generated by the views of Gewirth (see Beyleveld, 1991; Boylan, 1999).

Recently, the 2008 book of James Griffin, On Human Rights (2008) attempts to base human rights on autonomy and agency. Even though Griffin's overall view has key features common to the structural features of Gewirth, he does not agree with the Gewirth's goal of providing an argument for human rights that is logically inescapable.

Whilst starting the justification, granting a unique value to autonomy and human agency (called 'normative agency' by Griffin), within an agency-based approach making a place for a right to well-being and postulating certain abstract rights (well-being, freedom, and autonomy) are some of these common features.

Griffin is a strong supporter of seeing the human rights as fundamentally moral rights in the debate that currently exists between 'political' and 'orthodox' or 'moral' conceptions of human rights.

Griffin views the role of protecting the ability of people to purse and form conceptions of a life that is worthwhile as a defining one where he refers to this capacity as 'normative agency,' 'autonomy' and 'personhood.'

Such an ability to revise, form, and pursue conceptions that make a life worthwhile are seen to be of a paramount value being the basis of human rights whereby they are the exclusive source of human dignity (Griffin, 2008). According to Griffin this capacity is held very highly by people and perhaps it is even more that their happiness.

As per Griffin, human rights are also shaped by 'practicalities. 'Practicalities' have been defined by him as a 'second ground' of human rights.

By avoiding too many bends that are complicated, consulting facts about the nature of society and human nature and giving safety margins to the rights by enlarging them, they advise that the boundaries of rights be made clear. Whilst taking the practicalities into account, Griffin thus assigns the generic function of a protective normative agency to human rights.

As per Griffin, human rights become vulnerable to proliferation due to their suffering from an "indeterminacy of sense" which is more than for any other normative concepts. According to him, the best way to remedy this problem is to take account of practicalities and tie all human rights to the single value of normative agency.

"Ballooning of the content" of the rights that have been established and the invention of new human rights on a frequent basis has been criticized by him. All the same, the attitude of Griffin towards a majority of the rights in the UDHR is a friendly one.

Furthermore, many rights in interpersonal morality have been included in human rights by Griffin. For instance, according to Griffin a child's right to education is to be applied against the parents as well over and above being applicable against the government.

More than a description, the thesis propagated by Griffin that human rights are grounded in normative agency is a proposal of sorts being the best way in which human rights can be given coherence, unity, and limits.

However, a sharp line between the various other moral norms and human rights or effective barriers to the proliferation is unlikely to result by acceptance and following of this proposal. Griffin has himself recognized that the main reason behind this is that the normative agency 'generative capacities' are 'quite great.'

A series of rights would be required and a lot of threats shall be faced by these values in order to provide protection that is adequate with respect to the three components of normative agency (freedom, autonomy, and well-being).

5.6. POLITICAL CONCEPTIONS OF HUMAN RIGHTS

With regard to the function or role of human rights in the international political practice, there is a commitment of the Political Conception to understand human rights' distinctive nature. Different accounts have been offered by those who take up the Political Conception with regard to what the function or role comprises of.

As per Rawls, "human rights are a class of rights that play a special role in a reasonable Law of Peoples; they restrict the justifying reasons for war and its conduct; and they specify limits to a regime's internal autonomy."

For the society to have a good standing and be a member in a society of people that is reasonably just and is sufficient to exclude the intervention by the other people that is forceful and justified it is necessary that the society observes human rights.

According to Rawls, human rights are the conditions necessary of any system of social cooperation. When these are violated regularly, there is no cooperation of any kind, and a slave system or a command by force exists.

As per Rawl, a society cannot complain if its internal affairs are interfered with by external agents when it has failed to observe human rights for instance through coercive intervention or even though political or economic sanctions. Rawl's idea that limits are set to a society's internal autonomy by human rights finds support from Raz.

However, in two respects Raz's account differs from Rawl's. Firstly, Raz supports the view that human rights can be held against international organizations and agents of all kinds which includes groups, individuals, corporations, and other domestic institutions that are likely to cause a violation whereas human rights are primarily against states.

Secondly, according to Raz, Rawls has not succeeded in distinguishing between the limits of legitimate authority and the limits of sovereignty. As per Rawls for the social cooperation of any system, the necessary condition is the existence of human rights and he goes further in believing that the limits of sovereignty can be determined through the conditions of social cooperation.

At the same time, Raz postulates that a state cannot interfere with the affairs of another state whenever the latter exceeds its legitimate authority. For example, even if a state lacks internal legitimacy, it may still be protected from external interference from another state (where for instance corruption and bias envelope the external agents themselves).

In such cases, the limits of sovereignty cannot be defined solely by the conditions of social cooperation. According to Beitz in the current scene of international political practice, the role of human rights goes beyond the mere justification of foreign intervention or interference.

To take an example, guiding the practical judgments with respect to international concern or responsibility is encompassed in its broader role.

For example, rather than be classified as interference, certain measures are considered as assistance where a wide range of economic and political measures that is non-coercive can be used by the international organizations and states to influence the societies' internal affairs when human rights are being threatened.

Furthermore, as seen by Beitz, human rights give a reason to the non-governmental organizations and individuals whereby they can justifiably engage in political action that is oriented towards reform.

In other words, Beitz believes that rather than attributing a narrower view to the international role of human rights as seen by Rawl, it would be better to take a broader view especially from the point where the current human rights practices internationally are explained through the theory.

5.7. WHAT DOES IT MEANS TO VIOLATE HUMAN RIGHTS?

Every individual is entitled to enjoy certain rights that are basic irrespective of the circumstances and this fact has been universally accepted now. Certain political rights and civil liberties are included in this whereby the right to physical safety and life are the most fundamental ones.

The need for tolerance, justice, human dignity, and mutual respect in all the actions of the individuals has resulted in the articulation of human rights. The fact that the scope of justice and morality includes all individuals finds expression by speaking of rights.

Humane and a certain degree of decent treatment are ensured to all people through the protection of human rights. On the other hand, individuals are denied the most fundamental moral entitlements when the most basic human rights are violated.

It is equivalent to treating them as being less human and that they do not deserve dignity or respect. Various instances would include 'crimes against humanity' which comprise of torture, rape, slavery, genocide, medical experimentation or enforced sterilization and starving deliberately. An important part of the international law is to limit the power of the state that is unrestrained as most of the policies are implemented by the governments. The principle of non-discrimination and the notion that there is universal applicability to certain basic rights underlies the various laws whereby crimes against humanity are prohibited.

5.7.1. The Various Types of Violations

Tremendous amount of devastation is inflicted by conflicts even as large amounts of humanity suffer and the deaths resulting from the collateral damage caused by warfare and combat is but a small part. There is widespread assault on the fundamental right to life and on political rights over a period of protracted conflict.

Massacres, genocide, and entire populations being starved are some of the most severe violations of the right to life. The international extermination of a single racial, ethical, or religious group comprises genocide.

A group can be destroyed by killing group members, imposing measures to prevent birth, causing serious mental or bodily harm to them, or transferring children forcibly. The most offensive crime against humanity is genocide.

Women are marketed for prostitution and transported across national borders in a form of sexual slavery which is called trafficking. During war time, institutionalized sexual violence against women (VAW) takes on a new form of "comfort women."

At times, community, and male pride is seen to have been destroyed through sexual violence that brings about humiliation upon men who are unable to ensure the 'protection' of their women. It is also used to inflict terror amidst the overall population and silence strong women who are active politically.

As a part of the strategy of genocide, mass rapes may be inflicted whereby the conditions that are thus created bring about destruction of the entire group of people. During the 1990s for instance as reported by the media, as a part of a systematic and deliberate part to bring about victory in war, "rape and sexual atrocities" formed a part of the Bosnian Serb campaign in former Yugoslavia.

Programs of torture may be carried out by forces of the government rather than resorting to killing off the entire population. Psychological or physical torture may be inflicted whereby the aim is to humiliate or annihilate an individual's dignity. Mutilation, electric shocks to genitals, gums, and lips or beatings may be involved in physical torture. For long hours detainees are kept standing upright or they may be deprived of sleep, water or food and may even be tormented by noise of a very high-level in psychological torture.

Sometimes in order to extract information or confessions as well as to carry out interrogations, torture is used. In the current times torture has become a means of punishing political opponents whose ideology is different from that of the ruling party or for suppressing ideological and political dissent.

Additionally, each year thousands of people disappear from amongst the ones who have been detained owing to a connection with some conflicts whereby they are buried secretly after being killed. Forces of the government hold people in secret after taking them into custody and subsequently do not acknowledge or take the responsibility with respect to their fate or whereabouts.

Spreading of terror and securing information are the main reasons behind these abductions of individuals. A majority of times torture and threat is involved in interrogations resulting in the subsequent killing of those who have been arrested.

Towards the concealment of acts of summary execution and torture of the individuals who have been placed in custody, corpses are left at dumpsites or buried in unmarked graves. Families are more often than not unaware of the whereabouts of such people or even about the fact of their being alive.

Often, lesser forms of political oppressions are also enacted. Individuals are arrested arbitrarily and are either subject to trials that are grossly unfair or never brought to trial where they are a threat to the people sitting in seats of power.

Political participation of all kinds may be denied to mass groups of people whereby they are also denied the basic right to cast their vote. The freedom of movement of these people may be restricted through various measures. Mass expulsions, forcible relocations and denying the right to return to one's home or the right to asylum are some of these measures.

Discrimination may be another form of political oppression. On the basis of ethnicity, religion, gender, or race, there may be a denial of basic rights when this takes place. One of the severest forms of discrimination is apartheid via which race is made the basis for denying political rights.

Extreme forms of racial segregation were institutionalized in South Africa through the system of apartheid whereby laws prohibited sexual relations or marriages that were interracial and there was a requirement to live in different areas as per one's race.

Some individuals were regarded as lesser beings as per the law and were considered as inferior by definition. Social control was aimed at by the laws that were established under this system and racial lines were used to bring about a division in society bringing about a disregard for human rights in a systematic manner.

Over and above this, the vulnerability of women towards certain types of abuse with regard to human rights is quite high which is in addition to their sexual exploitation and abuse. In a large part of the world, discrimination is deeply woven into the fabric of that area which leads to many forms of oppressions in the social and political fields.

Basic liberties of women are severely restricted through harsh punishments for sexual "transgressions" and strict dress codes. Additionally, in many regions like Africa, the sufferance of women due to poverty is quite high compared to that of men and any kind of education, political influence, as well as job training is denied to them.

5.7.2. Human Rights Violations and Intractable Conflict

An interdependence which is quite strong exists between intractable conflicts and human rights violations as has been noted by many. Conflict is usually the result of an abuse of human rights which causes grave violations of human rights. Not surprisingly, abuse of human rights is rampant during war and for the purposes of resolving conflicts, it is essential to protect human rights.

At the root of many, a crisis is the violation of economic and political rights. When there is a denial of rights to adequate housing, food, cultural life and employment and exclusion of large groups of people from the decision-making processes of the society, social unrest is the likely result. In such conditions, the afflicted parties demand the meeting of their basic needs giving rise to justice conflicts.

Violations of human rights give rise to the spread of or the starting of many conflicts. To take an example, the determination of an adversary to continue fighting may be strengthened due to torture or massacres whereby hatred gets inflamed. The conflict may spiral out of control due to an increase in violence which may spring from the other side.

At the same time a wide range of rights are undermined by an armed conflict of any kind as most of the times it causes the civic institutions and infrastructure to breakdown. The right to adequate education and health are grossly threatened when schools and hospitals are closed.

Food shortage, poverty, and pollution are the most likely results of a collapse within the economic infrastructure. The right to self-determination is violated due to an economic oppression and breakdown of any kind which contributes towards more human tragedy taking the shape of starvation, sickness, and absence of basic shelter.

Civil rights are often denied when the government institutions suffer a breakdown which includes the right to freedom of movement, a fair trial, and privacy. In a large number of cases, there is rampant corruption in the judicial and police systems even as the government is seeing signs of increasing militarization.

This is often followed by detentions without trial, abductions, political executions, arbitrary arrests, torture, and assassinations.

Peace-building and reconciliation become very difficult where the human rights violations have been extreme. Peace negotiations can be badly hampered where the human rights issues have not been resolved.

When the memories of atrocity and severe violence are still fresh in the minds of the people on whom these have been afflicted, the parties are unable to move towards forgiveness and transformation of conflicts making the process of negotiations much more difficult.

5.7.3. What Can Be Done?

The enactment of international humanitarian law has been done to preserve humanity in all scenarios which includes conflicts as well. Even where conflicts are rampant, such laws create a sphere of peace calling for dialogue and imposing the principle of a humanity that is common to all.

Total war or unlimited force is ruled out by this law via which the use of violence is sought to be limited whereby hoping that the necessary conditions can be created so that peace may return. Reporting of any violations and monitoring compliance with human rights standards is ensured though various international committees.

On the occurrence of a breach, the matter is tried in a war crimes tribunal or an international court or brought forth to an international tribunal.

However, at times, conflicts reach such a stage that they cannot be helped by the international law. Resorting to a legal path no longer remains an option when the number of victims keeps increasing and a bigger number is taken in as prisoners subjecting them to torture or execution.

Furthermore, a reconciliation of the safeguards with subject to human rights and resolution of conflicts is often a difficult task. Protection of human rights and providing help to parties in order to bring about the resolution of a conflict has failed in many initiatives aimed at conflict-prevention as well as peacekeeping.

A major reason for this is that within the state's wars have escalated even though between states there has been a reduction in the number of wars. There is a drastic increase in organized violence in many internal conflicts.

Within the 'internal' conflicts, a central part of the warfare includes crimes against humanity, aggression against civilians and genocide. Identity issues are often the cause of such violence-the out-group/in-group dynamics—and the attempts made by one group to maintain and gain political control to the exclusion of other on the basis of religious or ethnic factors.

The focus in such conflicts is on the differences and ideas or principles do not form the basis of these conflicts. The violations of human rights dehumanize the 'outsiders' taking the form of ethnic cleaning or discrimination which are made feasible psychologically. Such internal conflicts often have attacks on human rights at their very core.

Organized violence needs to be controlled by the public authorities by regaining the control with respect to such situations. Additionally, to defuse exclusivist ideas more democratic and inclusive values are required. Human rights and international legal norms need to be championed by the leaders in light of such violations.

In order to promote mutual respect and tolerance within a society and maintaining a civil society, such attitudes should be brought about in people by making human rights the central factor.

However, when the individuals who are in power bring about violations of human rights, it only results in grave difficulties. Outside intervention then becomes necessary to bring about a stop to such abuse.

5.8. RESPONSIBILITIES OF POLITICAL PARTIES

Human rights often outline the responsibilities and roles that are to be performed by political parties especially in a democracy where they are equally responsible for ensuring the human rights system is both incorporated and followed in a democratic set up.

An important role is played by the political parties along with the other actors of the civil society towards the promotion and monitoring of human rights. This would include the following subsections.

5.8.1. Consultations and Hearings on Law and Policy Projects Which Are Related to Human Rights

Media, campaign, and consultations are some of the ways via which political parties can tender their opinion with respect to law projects and new policies.

5.8.2. Dissemination of Human Rights Related Information

Specific categories of persons or human rights issues may be focused upon by political parties as a part of their campaigns or policies and disseminate information about their situation, status or human rights using the medium of campaigns, media or participation in information meetings.

5.8.3. Human Rights Monitoring

Human rights violations may be denounced by political parties or they may highlight issues of human rights thus participating in the monitoring actions of the state with regard to human rights in an informal manner.

As such, political parties have no legal obligations with regard to human rights as they are not a part of the state within a democratic set-up. All the same, at times, there may be direct or indirect participation of political parties in the country's ruling.

When members of a political party get appointed or elected to form a part of the government or parliament, they become closely associated in the exercising of power which is of a political nature.

Political parties and members thereof then become a part of the infrastructure of the state and they become duty bound to protect human rights within the human rights system of the nation or state.

As far as political parties are concerned, it basically entails that they are encouraged to:

5.8.4. Combat Violence in Action and Speech

Within a democratic system, the use of violence must be rejected by political parties for the furtherance of political goals. Own militias should not be maintained by them nor should violence be advocated or resorted to buy them along with a total refusal to use hate speech as a political tool.

Resorting to or inciting violence is punishable by law in many countries. Such a legal framework should not only be in place but the political parties must also ensure that its effective implementation is done in all situations and that all their actions respect it.

5.8.5. Support Political Pluralism

The coexistence within a society of a diversity of political organizations and political opinions is entailed in the right to freedom of expression and the right to freedom of association. This must be respected by all private players and the state should both encourage and protect it.

This also implies that any act of the political parties that hampers the creation of other political parties should not be followed by them. An enabling framework should be brought in place so that the free operation and creation of political parties is secured through the combined efforts of the state and the political parties.

Additionally, there should be healthy discussions and debates amongst different political parties. The right to free speech with respect to the opposing parties should not be hindered nor should their meetings be disrupted by them.

5.8.6. Combat Discrimination

At the very core of human rights is the principle of non-discrimination. Anti-discriminatory legislation and equality must be followed by the political parties as well as their members.

This entails that ether shall be no discrimination either with respect to inclusion and hiring of new people to work within the party or with respect to their external relationships. Equality legislation which includes aspects like gender quota for electoral list must be followed whilst nomination election candidates.

5.8.7. Human Rights Screening to Be Undertaken With Respect to New Proposed Legislations and Policies

Whenever new policies are proposed or the government is considering proposals in the parliament or new legislative measures are, being considered it is imperative that compliance with human rights is considered by the political parties themselves.

This essentially means that human rights are kept paramount when laws are undertaken and policies are developed in a way that promotes and protects human rights resulting in policies that are compliant with the rights (Figure 5.5).

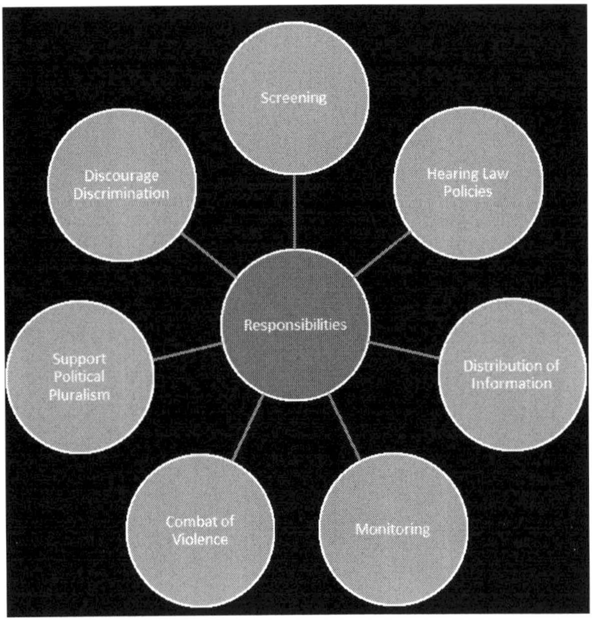

Figure 5.5: Responsibilities of political parties.

5.9. CONCLUSION

Human rights are the basic rights without which the very existence of humans becomes questionable. In the recent years, human rights have been widely recognized and accepted as essential to all individuals. Various international bodies have been established that help to create, support, and promote these rights.

Over and above their creation, violation thereof is also looked upon strictly by the international community. International courts, tribunals, and treaties ensure that these rights are not only complied with but in case of a violation, action can be taken against the offending party.

Armed conflict which can be both external as well as internal is one of the main causes for the violation of human rights. An increase in conflicts within the states has only brought about an escalation in the violation of such rights. There is an important responsibility on the political parties to abjure from acts which violate human rights of individuals as well as those of the opposing parties that may have conflicting views.

REFERENCES

1. Beetham, D., (1995). Introduction: Human rights in the study of politics. *Political Studies*, [online] *43*(1), pp. 1–9. Available at: https://onlinelibrary.wiley.com/doi/pdf/10.1111/j.1467–9248.1995.tb01696.x (accessed on 25 April 2020).
2. Lagoutte, S., & Petersen, M., (2018). *Political Parties and Human Rights*. [eBook] Danish Institute for Human Rights. Available at: https://menneskeret.dk/sites/menneskeret.dk/files/media/dokumenter/udgivelser/forskning_2018/political-parties-and-human-rights-2018.pdf (accessed on 25 April 2020).
3. Liao, S., & Etinson, A., (n.d.). *Political and Naturalistic Conceptions of Human Rights. A False Polemic?* [eBook] Available at: http://www.smatthewliao.com/wp-content/uploads/2012/06/LiaoEtinsonPoliticalAndNaturalisticConceptionsOfHumanRights.pdf (accessed on 25 April 2020).
4. Maiese, M., (2003). *Human Rights Violations*. [online] Beyond intractability. Available at: https://www.beyondintractability.org/essay/human_rights_violations (accessed on 25 April 2020).
5. n.d. *Chapter 2: Human Rights Background*. [eBook] Available at: https://www.theadvocatesforhumanrights.org/uploads/ch_2_2.pdf (accessed on 25 April 2020).
6. Plato.stanford.edu. (2019). *Human Rights*. [online] Available at: https://plato.stanford.edu/entries/rights-human/ (accessed on 25 April 2020).
7. Un.org. (n.d.). *Human Rights*. [online] Available at: https://www.un.org/en/sections/issues-depth/human-rights/ (accessed on 25 April 2020).

Chapter 6

The Culture of Corruption: Taking the World Back

CONTENTS

The culture of corruption highlights the different forms of corruption prevailing in our society for decades. This article talks about how corruption hinders the overall growth of the country by planting the seeds in every aspect. One of the most common ways of corruption is Bribery' which is tough to eradicate.

Different forms of corruption such as political corruption, business corruption, corruption in judiciary, etc. have been briefly discussed as to how it weakens the backbone of the country. In light, Corruption leads to many biased decisions that have weakened the efficiency and effectiveness of the public sector.

Further, it has been briefly stated that the country will eventually lose its credibility and legitimacy if basic public services are not delivered to the citizens due to corruption. This article also talks about how media can be easily silenced through bribes from the circumvented rules and regulations which causes illicit money flows and political crises from weak public budget control.

This shows the signs of a poor democracy. In the end, the article talks about how the government officials as well as common people takes the easy way out to achieve success by spreading the disease in the form of corruption which will ultimately take back the country.

6.1. INTRODUCTION

Dishonest conduct popularly known with the name "Corruption" has been commonly and continuously been used in our society and also, is occurring in all civilizations. However, this phenomenon has been seriously exposed in the last 20 years.

Corruption has its very own unique way to spread fraudulent conduct and the way it has been shaped it made quite a larger impact on the economy and the society. Among the most common reason behind corruption includes the political as well as economic environment, professional ethics and morality and, obviously, habits, tradition, customs, and demography (Figure 6.1).

Figure 6.1: Corruption is a major hurdle in politics.

Source: Image by Wikipedia.

The way it has been affecting the economy (and also on the wider society) is a topic to be researched well. Yet this has not been researched completely. Therefore, the corruption tends to hinder the economic growth and also, tends to affect business operations, employment, and investments.

Tax revenue has been reduced on a larger scale and it has affected various financial assistance programs. A high degree of corruption has been shaped by the wider society in context of lowering of trust in the law as well as the rule of law, education, and also, the quality of life (which includes access to infrastructure, health care).

However, an unambiguous answer does not exist as to how to deal with corruption. There can be something that works in one country or one region and it is not necessary that it will be successful in another.

6.2. DEFINITIONS OF CORRUPTION

Over the years, corruption has become the multi-faceted phenomenon that has received some of the different exposition some of them rather restricted, similar to those comparing it with bribe taking, and a portion of a progressively broad nature and frequently having solid good undercurrents.

Extended as much that even the concept is applied to the social class, a social body, and also, the historical era. Such uncertainty of meaning contributes to explaining why measuring corruption is problematic.

This is the much observed difficulty for which there can be one other obvious reason and that is the constant prevailing of corrupt activities. This means that in most of the cases the possibility of the area of criminal justice is not revealed by their perpetrators.

Nevertheless, with such inherent difficulties, the task of measuring corruption is very instructive. On the one side, it provides access to a measure of our ignorance, and motivation for prudence trying to assess its level and, even more so, how it may change with the time.

Corruption may be defined as the abuse of entrusted power for private gain. It captures three elements of corruption:

1. Public and private sectors
2. Abuse of power
3. Benefit

On the other side, and possibly, more importantly, it anticipates the route in order to organize our thoughts according to the phenomenon of corruption entirely and also, to propose a concepts related to corruption including both legal and illegal.

There are some specific examples which have studied that the corruption should not be considered as a perversion of governance. It has been considered as one of its constituent characteristics and, sometimes, as one of its key instruments albeit, one which is very nocuous to society as a whole.

Corruption can be portrayed and arranged in various manners. There is one of the most predominant sorts or classifications of corruption and that is the supply versus, ordinary versus unusual corruption, terrific versus unimportant corruption, demand corruption and open versus private corruption.

There are few other categories or ways of describing corruption such as systemic versus individual or isolated, corruption by commission versus by omission, by the degree of coercion used to perform the illegal act, and the way it has been benefited.

Supply-side corruption is used in order to provide clarification regarding the demonstration of offering an unlawful installment or undue preferred position, whereas demand-side corruption direct towards the acceptance or solicitation of such a payment or advantage.

The two major terms-active and passive corruptions that has been used synonymously with a huge corruption demand and supply. Usually, the conventional corruption occurs when government officials, whether they are ranked higher or lower, illegitimately receive or acquire an undue advantage for their personal use, disregarding public interest.

Conventional corruption consists of an element of reciprocity that is the adjuration and the acceptance of bribes (supply as well as demand bribery) that functions within and therefore considered as the forms of conventional corruption.

Nevertheless, the unconventional corruption tends to exist whenever either a public or government official acts without considering the public's interest. Their main goal is to attain a specific and personal gain. However, there is a key element that states that there is no existence of relationship of reciprocity, because of the fact that there is no clear-cut transaction in between both the parties.

Forms of corruption can vary but it also includes acts. The misappropriation, theft, embezzlement, and breach of trust are all included in these acts. Grand and petty corruption is both subcategories of conventional corruption. Sometimes, the petty corruption is equated with bureaucratic corruption. This means that there is involvement of public administration officials and also, some of the non-elected officials are also involved (Figure 6.2).

Figure 6.2: There are several laws that discourage corruption.

Source: Image by Pixabay.

The petty corruption is used and this includes bribes which are paid to enforcement officials, customs personnel, health service providers, and other government officials. Facilitation payments, which are commonly known as grease payments, fall under this category.

There are some grand corruption which includes someone who misuses the opportunities which are assigned through government work, it can be higher-ranking government officials and elected officials. Thus, the consequence of bribes offered or paid in connection with large-scale government projects includes infrastructure and construction projects.

Political corruption is considered to be as grand corruption and the reason is its seriousness and the involvement of high-ranking public officials. It exists where trusted politicians and government agents with enforcing laws are themselves corrupt.

It usually occurs at the top levels of government. There is another type of grand corruption and this includes State capture. This can be characterized as a company or organization which tends to shape and influence legislation or government policies in the whole sector (e.g., the extractive as well as mining industry or taxation) through payments.

Contrastingly, there can be adverse effect wherein the public officials try to manipulate actors who are in the private sector for their gain, specifically known as reversed State capture. There is a not-so-distant equivalent of state capture which is known as influence corruption, and for them, actors, and goals is similar.

The absence of any such payment, advantage, or transaction ever taking place brings a major difference. In this situation, influence is exerted on the basis of the ability of organization in order to impact policy. This is the result of its ownership, its size, potential ties, and interactions with the State officials.

The public or private nature is other ways to characterize the phenomena of corruption. The distinction lays in the divisions in which work the members of the unlawful demonstration. Any public official is involved in the public corruption where one party to the corrupt act and the public official can be domestic or foreign. On the other hand, the private corruption involves only individuals in the private sector (which is why it is sometimes called private-to-private corruption).

Amidst public corruption, legislation can be distinguished by the type of public official it targets; it does not matter whether the official is a domestic public official or a foreign public official. When a particular private company shows corrupt Behavior, its clients, and suppliers have the surveillance to reach out to the competitors if corruption is noticed.

However, it is not the same with the government-owned company as taxpayers and citizens can't depend on different associations to give similar taxpayer driven organizations, for example, social insurance, or open security. The degree of the imposing business model of the good or service provided, in this manner, influences the apparent danger.

A whole world is created by the public corruption where there exists connection between the states versus society relationships. Corruption is everywhere; its existence can be seen in private businesses and individuals in a number of different forms, and that too without involving the government officials or agencies.

Some instances of corrupt acts in the private sector may include bribing, swindling, and mafia-methods. As the public and private sectors are more and more twisted as a consequence of outsourcing, privatization, and rapid growth in the private sector in some of the countries. The growing influence of multinational corporations and State-owned enterprises has demarcated a line between public and private funds. Systemic corruption can be seen where corruption is pervasive or entrenched in society. In other words, it exists where a routine dealing between the government and private individuals or businesses takes place.

In such cases, tension arises between formal and informal rules, as there are solid impetuses for individuals, public officials, businesses, and individuals in order to comply with the illegitimate system. On the contrary, there exists the isolated or individual corruption in the case when corruption is rare or it contains a few individual acts. The acts of corruption can further be carried out by commission, but also by omission.

A public official can either maintain a strategic distance from to act or act in the presentation of their obligations, in return for a profit by an individual or business. These elements, just as the level of pressure applied by the public official and the sort of advantage allocated (money related, physical great, or obtaining a social commitment), are worth noting because of the fact that they may influence dynamic and legitimization by degenerate on-screen characters.

The equivalent can be said in situations where the type of advantage got isn't prompt yet rather the consequence of the formation of a social commitment. People may be less inclined to take part in degenerate Behavior in situations where the partner or offering is a money related advantage, contrasted with more subtle advantages, for example, future favors or services.

6.3. TYPES OF CORRUPTION

1. Corruption in judiciary.
2. Political corruption.
3. Business corruption.
4. Corruption in education.
5. Corruption in law enforcement.
6. Administrative corruption.
7. Corruption in government.
8. Health care system (Figure 6.3).

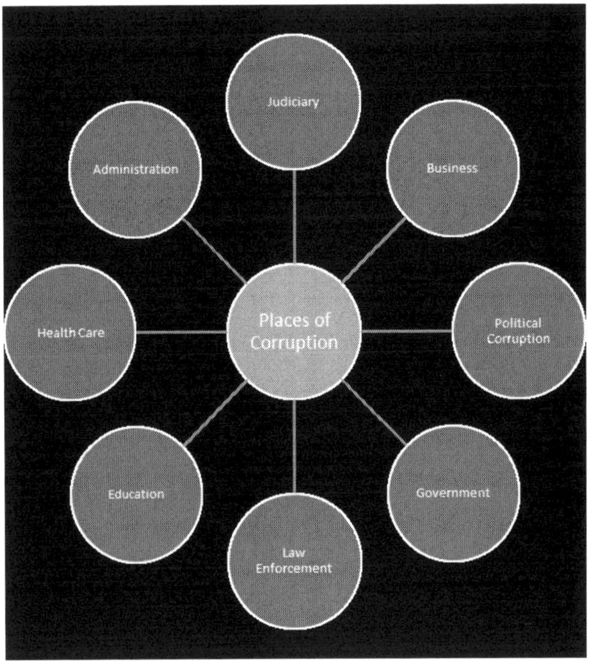

Figure 6.3: Kinds of corruptions that exist in society.

6.3.1. Types of Corruption in the Judiciary

Among the most dominant pillars of the constitution of the nation, one is Judiciary. This works in order to safeguard the citizens. But, the judges in the courts are likely susceptible to corruption because of the unlimited power that they have. The unfavorable situation forces them to destroy the justice as well as the judiciary support to a person or society as a whole. The most common types of corruption in the judiciary are:

- Delayed justice;
- Selective justice;
- Voluntary harassment;
- Scope for misuse and misbehavior.

1. **Delayed Justice:** There is a judiciary phrase known as justice delayed is justice denied. The application of the principle is done by the judiciary in a few countries. Considering most of the cases, it can be said that the victim falls prey so as to suffer because of the delay of injustice.

This occurs in both criminal cases as well as civil cases. Some cases are dragged for a prolonged period even though the case was meant to be settled down much faster. This certainly involves suffering to the persons involved in the cases.

Some prolonged cases lead to common man waiting for justice often suffers severe mental stress and die of it. This delay in many ways could be due to the intentionally dragging of cases by the judges. If the closing stage is reached in a case, then they tend to postpone the judgment in order to deliver after court holidays.

In the opinion of the judge, it could be seen as a vacation. But, for those who are involved, it would be seen as an unexpected nightmare. They have spent time in anxiety and mental suffering with the outcome of the verdict.

2. **Selective Justice:** This is an even funny way of misuse of the justice system. When there are a number of cases which are pending, then they take up cases in a flash to give bail or different reliefs to the rich and renowned individuals. Be that as it may, there will be numerous average folks trusting that their case will be heard. That is where our country lacks behind while discriminating between the rich and the poor in every sphere of life.
3. **Voluntary Harassment:** This usually occurs when the people in the system have a political or religious direction. They try to give orders out of their discomfort, past hatred or based on their personal opinions to satisfy their self-esteem. You may notice that some judgment would be targeted against a political party or a religious community.
4. **Scope for Misuse and Misbehavior:** In some cases, bribe comes into the playfield where judicial officials take huge bribe in exchange try to relive a person from a long-term punishment. This is not a secret and the use of the right channel helps one to achieve that until unless there is no look out from the public.

6.3.2. Corruption in Business

The corruption in business is considered to be a widespread and also, a long-standing problem for a large number of years. Business people choose the path of corrupt practices to generate more into their pockets. They can do so by forcing the government to enact some laws in their favor.

Another way is to avoid quality control in order to produce sub-standard goods and also, to save money. Let's take an example of US. There is Affordable Care Act in the United States, and according to this act, everyone is required to have health insurance. If they do not have the same then they are required to pay a penalty.

So, in this way law is enforced to support insurance companies. Further, it helps to produce sub-standard products, the lack of stringent quality control enables to businessmen to sell low-quality goods. But the same company tends to produce a high standard as well as high quality product for other countries with powerful quality control laws.

6.3.3. Political Corruption

This is perhaps the worst case of moral corruption. Here political parties come into play and have its certain ways to do it like:

1. Appease people by either freebies or subsidies.
2. Appease minorities.
3. Buy votes and mandate.

Persistence of any type of political corruption is a failure to the nation. As a result, a large number of people are unable to read the intention that the politicians have and then, they fall in their trap and provide them with their votes.

6.3.4. Corruption in Government

In this, the corruption is done by those who are in power. They do unfair means by making scams, awarding contracts to their friends, etc. This will continue until the end of the term in office.

The media who is the fourth pillar of our society can easily track their dirty politics and let the public know it. However, this is not the way how things work out because there is few media bodies also which are corrupted; they protect the government officials by acting blindly in response to crucial issues.

6.3.5. Corruption in Law Enforcement

This type of corruption usually takes place in police departments. Corruption in law enforcement is present in almost all countries. The police authorities accept bribes and help destroy the evidence.

6.3.6. Corruption in Education

Education is one of the valuable needs of a common man and should be kept away from dirty tactics. However, Corruption has expanded to all spheres of life. So, to encase them, there are many businessmen in the education sector. They tend to take a bribe to offer seats for undeserving students and let them admit in higher colleges.

6.3.7. Corruption in the Health Care System

This includes improper healthcare or even it includes favor to one company or also, some of the related corruption. However, in developed countries corruption can be rarely seen or witness.

6.3.8. Administrative Corruption

The administrative form of corruption is somewhat same like the government-based corruption. However, it is spread among the public servants to the lower levels also. There are officers or servants who can be involved in the bribery in order to perform their duties towards to common public.

There are different types of corruption on the basis of the consequences and these include:

- Those with no loss to the public but for one individual or group;
- Those with a loss to the public;
- Those without any loss to others.

Let's see the three types in detail:

1. **Those Having Loss to the Public:** These are corruption cases that cause a large amount of loss to the public. In the world, these are considered to be highly prevalent and the reason is that the common people and the innocent people are not active enough to question them or fight against them.

For example, a company takes up a natural resource in a country and its intention is to exploit them for the purpose of national benefit. Once they procure the rights to utilize the asset, they don't do it to maximum capacity and adequately. At the point when the administration attempts to address them, these individuals handle those authorities by either giving financial advantages or giving crazy reasons. Additionally, they attempt to move the activity position of honest officials by using higher influences.

Also, when persons are randomly stopped for checking the license.

Majority of the time, if a person is caught having no credible certificates, and then the bribe is offered to the officials to let them go. There are chances that such unlicensed drivers can further cause accidents to the common public. Therefore, here the corruption affects loss to the public and also, affect loss to the whole country.

2. **Those with No Loss to the Public but for One Individual or Group:** These types of cases occur to a company or a group or family at the point when they are abused by others. Assuming a family is in advantage of or having a property and in they contracted it a third individual. After certain long stretches of utilization, the outsider will not stop the property and when addressed attempts to get official help by them and get the family far from the property with their help.

Another occasion is a young lady or somebody who is assaulted or murdered, and the police attempt to see that the body of evidence against the guilty party flops because of absence of proof, and so forth. Here the young lady or her family is in distress and not the mass public.

3. **Those with No Loss to Anyone Else Including Public:** These cause technically no loss to the public. This happens in the case when a benefit is provided to an official for properly performing his duty. Let's take an example of developing countries. In those countries, the government workforce is not much disciplined. They take months or even years so that they can pass a file or complete any task.

If the person who is concerned gives, a small monetary benefit or even small bribe to the official then the process gets obstructed. The concerned person who gave a bribe does not lose much. But the official gets some of the benefit which is not much huge (Table 6.1).

Table 6.1: Categories of Corruption

Categories of Corruption	Description
Bribery	The act of dishonestly persuading someone to act in one's favor by a payment or other inducement. Inducements can take the form of gifts, loans, fees, rewards or other advantages (taxes, services, donations, etc.). The use of bribes can lead to collusion (e.g., inspectors under-reporting offences in exchange for bribes) and/or extortion (e.g., bribes extracted against the threat of over-reporting).

Embezzlement	To steal, misdirect or misappropriate funds or assets placed in one's trust or under one's control. From a legal point of view, embezzlement need not necessarily be or involve corruption.
Facilitation payment	A small payment, also called a "speed" or "grease" payment, made to secure or expedite the performance of a routine or necessary action to which the payer has legal or other entitlement.
Fraud	The act of intentionally and dishonestly deceiving someone in order to gain an unfair or illegal advantage (financial, political or otherwise).
Collusion	An arrangement between two or more parties designed to achieve an improper purpose, including influencing improperly the actions of another party.
Extortion	The act of impairing or harming, or threatening to impair or harm, directly or indirectly, any party or the property of the party to influence improperly the actions of a party.
Patronage, clientelism and nepotism	Patronage at its core means the support given by a patron. In government, it refers to the practice of appointing people directly.

Source: https://assets.publishing.service.gov.uk/government/uploads/system/uploads/attachment_data/file/406346/corruption-evidence-paper-why-corruption-matters.pdf.

6.4. THE NATURE OF THE TRANSACTION

A second taxonomic approach differentiates corruption based on certain aspects of the transaction. There are several schemes which have been developed along these lines. One rather simple approach links the corrupt influence direction. It distinguishes bribery from extortion. In bribery, societal interests use extra-legal payments or bribes to influence the content of state policy or its implementation.

Considering a broader side of the more systemic level, it can be said that this form of corrupt influence tend to take on the characteristics of state capture. It is the point where an entire agency or institution operates on behalf of societal interests. On the other hand, extortion includes using and abusing the state power by the public officials in order to demand extra-legal payments or rents in response to provide a legitimate or illegitimate service.

In blackmail, the heading of impact streams from state to society. In any case, in pay off, the heading is switched. It is very peculiar when sedate dealers have a large portion of the police on their finance doing their offering versus when the police investigation negligible hoodlums or bribe from residents without a doubt or envisioned offenses.

Syed Alatas (1990, cited in Heywood 1997, 42526) offered another and more elaborated approach on the basis of the aspects of the corrupt transaction. Furthermore, he specified seven forms of corruption.

1. **Transactive Corruption:** This involves the mutual arrangement done between a donor and a recipient.
2. **Supportive Corruption:** This refers to acts which are designed in order to protect and strengthen existing corruption.
3. **Defensive Corruption:** This type refers to the act the victim of extortion is compelled to engage in;
4. **Extortive Corruption:** This implies some form of compulsion usually harming a party;
5. **Investive Corruption:** This includes an act with no immediate payoff, but sometimes an understanding of a favor in the future;
6. **Autogenic Corruption:** This entails one person acting alone having no official-citizen exchange; and
7. **Nepotistic Corruption:** This type relates to family members being appointed to positions in the government;

A typology is the third approach based on the characteristics of the transaction. The variation can be seen from the relative size and frequency of the acts. Usually, this distinction is expressed in terms of grand versus petty corruption.

Ultimately, the grand corruption involves enormous aggregates of cash and normally fewer regular exchanges, while at the opposite end insignificant defilement alludes to littler and increasingly routine installments. This qualification will in general equal courses for those established in the institutional situation of the state official included.

Again, the grand corruption is required to happen among elevated level government authorities who have restricted cooperation with the general population, while insignificant debasement will, in general, occur among low-level, bureaucratic laborer's who normally connect with people in general.

6.4.1. Systemic Framework

A systematic framework is somewhat related to differences based on size and frequency. However, there are some distinctions often based on the broader pattern of corruption within the system. This approach focuses on the individual corrupt act as well as highlights the context in which the occurrence of the act takes place.

For example, Mark Robinson (1988) identifies three forms of corruption which include:

- **First is Incidental Corruption:** This is confined to malfeasance on part of the individual and thus, it is rare.
- **Second, Institutional Corruption:** It refers to the certain institutions that may be riddled with corruption largely due to the absence of controls.
- **Third and the Last is Systemic Corruption:** This type reflects the situations where corruption is deeply rooted and pervasive throughout society.

A similar kind of distinction contradicts centralized and decentralized corruption on the basis of the level of control which is exercised by the political elite over local officials (Bardhan, 2006, p. 344).

This is the approach parallels other distinctions as well. For instance, it can be said that the institutional, systemic, and centralized corruption usually involves elaborated webs and chains of illegal payoffs that occurs inside the government, often to the benefit of superiors or the political party.

6.4.2. Motive or Purpose

Another approach that distinguishes corruption relies on the purpose, motives, or results of the corrupt act. Obviously, the range can be extensive.

Another theory that distinguishes motive separates corruption that proceeds on purely personal interests from the corruption that benefits a clique, a political party, or an institution which can be more systematic.

For instance, considering the analysis that is done in between organized crime and corruption, Margaret Beare (1997) provided a non-exhaustive taxonomy of corruption on the basis of motive or outcome majorly.

She classifies into four different types:

- **Bribes/Kickbacks:** These are paid or even demanded in response to providing permission to do legitimate business;
- **Protection Corruption:** In this the payments are done in exchange for providing permission to engage in illegitimate business;
- **Election/Campaign Corruption:** This is designed in order to make sure continuation of the influence; and

- **Systemic Top-Down Corruption:** In this, the wealth of the nation is systematically siphoned off by the ruling elites.

6.4.3. Theoretical Linkages and Methodological Challenges

There are a number of theories which identify different forms of corruption and here, some are based on the norms, the institutional location of the participants, the underlying motives, or even the nature of the transaction. It is largely helpful to such an extent that it enhances our theoretical understanding of corruption (Gerring, 1999).

But one thing is for sure that it hinders the growth of the country. A significant part of the corruption writing investigating the fundamental causes and outcomes of corruption failure leads to separate types of Corruption, at the end of the day, is commonly seen as a particular class of political conduct.

Specifically, this is valid for the greater part of the quantitative, cross-national examinations on account of the manner in which defilement is typically estimated. From one perspective, contention can be raised that the political corruption of any stripe facilitates all or other types of corruption and that all types of corruption stem from similar causes.

There can be many reasons for corruption considering being equivalent in each part of degenerated exercises. A few factors, for example, leniency or resilience, the absence of trust or social capital or even the absence of vote based system, for example, would appear to take care of bureaucratic defilement similar to the political debasement, pay off just as coercion, defilement inside the police, the legal executive, and the gatherings, endlessly.

It is indeed a fact that formal models show that corrupt activity generally depends on how much corrupt activity is taking place within the society, furthermore, suggesting a common pattern (Bardhan, 2006; Mishra, 2006).

Such type of assertion results in grouping of different forms of corruption together. This justifies the use of crude as well as composite measures of the phenomenon and also, it sustains the search for a common set of causal factors and also, consequences which are unified or one-dimensional.

On the flipped side, there is another theory floating around which suggests that there are a number of different forms of corruption which may not necessarily go together. In addition to this, it suggests that there are certain factors which can relate only to some specific types of corruption and not others. So, the cause may not be similar every time. For example, Mocan (2004) and Morris (2008) find weak as well as limited correlations which connect the perceptions of corruption from actual involvement while paying bribes or being asked in order to pay a bribe, specifically among some of the developing countries.

For example, as per the observations of Mocan (2004), when the quality of the institution (that is measured by the risk of expropriation) is controlled for, the weak association between corruption and corruption perception disappears.

Bardhan (2006) goes with a different approach that differentiates the bureaucratic from political corruption and furthermore, finds that in the case of the United States, the two do not go well together. It also finds that the United States suffers high levels of political corruption, but on the other side, it has low levels of bureaucratic corruption.

There was a theory presented by Michael Johnston (2005) which was based on the work of corruption syndromes. In other words, it highlights different causes for different patterns of corruption.

Throwing the parity of financial chances and political chances, frail or solid-state and common society as key causal operators, Johnston watched four disorders of debasement intrigue bunch offering, tip-top authority, divided support and support machines that contrast related to the basic causal specialists, the examples or the types of defilement inside the general public, in the ramifications for the political framework, and thus on the methodologies expected to control debasement.

There is a correlation drawn for debasement in Latin America, Daniel Gingerich (2009) correspondingly interfaces various kinds of relative portrayal (PR) constituent frameworks to unmistakable classes of defilement. The open-list, PR system found in Brazil will, in general, make solid motivating forces for officials to gather an individual after by conveying pork and private merchandise to supporters back home by means of, to some extent, defilement.

Yet, while the open-list PR system in Brazil takes care of individual plans of debasement to pay for costly close to home political races, the shut rundown PR framework found in Argentina and Bolivia encourages an alternate example of defilement, where the intensity of the gathering first-class, combined with a more politicized administration, pushes party pioneers to hit manages civil servants and channel open assets to support the gathering.

A slightly different theoretical approach connects distinct forms of corruption to different perceptions which enlighten the seriousness or level of corruptness by the elite and the public. Arnold Heidenheimer (1970) in his earliest observation explored the connection of the perception of corruptness to the nature of obligations that exists in the society.

A similar approach was explored by John Peters and Susan Welch (1978). They used the opinion data in order to find that the acts involving a non-political official (judge instead of a politician), a public role (instead of a private citizen), donations from constituents instead of the non-constituents and large payoffs are being deemed in much serious way.

There is a most recent study done in France by Lascoumes and Tomescu-Hatto (2008). This study gauges the level of corruption considering a large number of different corrupt acts. Moreover, this enables the researchers so as to differentiate between the four groups of citizens on the basis of their different perceptions of the degree of tolerance for some for the specific acts of favoritism (whether condemn or not) and entire perception of the extent of corruption that exists in the public officials.

Methodological has been considered tough in studying different forms of corruption. Although there exists a number of taxonomies and typologies which are developed by analysts, there is still lack of the tools in order to adequately measure the various classes of corruption.

Today, Corruption Perception Index provided by Transparency International (TI) is referred to as the most commonly used measure empirical work in order to explore the causes or consequences of corruption. However, this indicator is one-dimensional and does not differentiate among types or forms of corruption (Johnston, 2005, p. 19).

While it has significantly enhanced the study, the use of crude as well as one-dimensional measures of corruption cannot deliver questions which are identified with the number of different types of corruption. It may not be sufficient essentially to state that a province endures broad or foundational debasement, or to anticipate that the equivalent causal components should lie behind all types of defilement or for all to apply a comparable effect.

Tragically, at this stage, this might be all that institutionalized proportions of corruption can let us know and all that we can gain from a worldwide point of view. There is recognition with respect to how it estimated through assessments of public sentiment, TI's progressively intricate Corruption

Barometer differentiates corruption by institutional area. This provides a significant methodological tool to differentiate countries based not only on the overall level of corruption but on different patterns of corruption. Some section of the theoretical challenge is to use this data in order to test as well as polish the theories which differentiates the cause and consequence, further moving the study beyond its one-dimensional focus.

6.5. THE RATIONALE FOR FIGHTING CORRUPTION

Corruption tends to weaken the bone of sustainable political, economic, and social development, for developing, emerging, and developed economies alike. Private sector productivity gets in danger due to corruption while setting incentives in order to allocate resources to the activities which are not productive and moreover, by deterring innovation as well as the emergence of new companies.

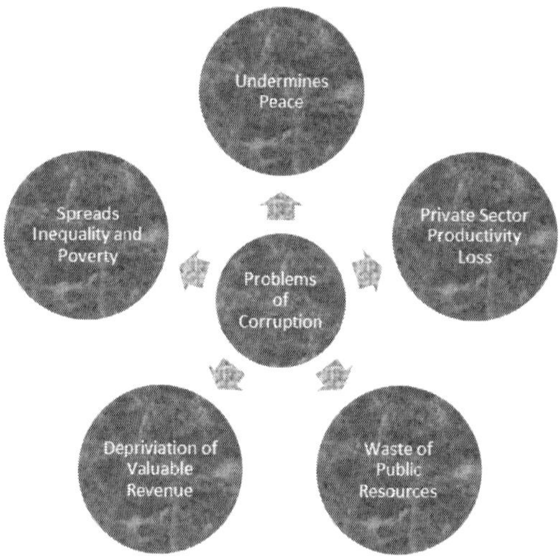

Figure 6.4: Various reasons to fight corruption.

Corruption leads to many biased decisions that hinder public sector productivity in public expenditures. This can be done by impairing the skills and also, the professionalism of the civil service and furthermore by reduction of the public resources which are available in order to provide support productivity in the economy. And corruption debilitates the comprehensive development of the nation by undermining the chances to take an interest similarly in social, financial, and political life and also, tends to affect the dispersion of pay and prosperity. Corruption additionally disintegrates trust in government and open foundations, rendering change progressively troublesome (Figure 6.4).

6.5.1. Corruption Reduces Private Sector Productivity

Corruption one way or another tends to raise the cost of doing business because the bribes and drawn-out negotiate them to bargain, and this add costs to a business transaction. According to the OECD Foreign Bribery Report, bribes are around 10.9% of the value of a transaction and also, are 34.5% of profits (OECD, 2014a).

Corruption acts as two sides of the same coin because it tends to create uncertainty. This is due to the fact that there can always be a competing firm which is willing to offer a higher bribe so as to tilt the business in his/her favor. By bringing down productivity and raising vulnerability, corruption will in general dishearten the passage of remote players and accordingly the advantages of rivalry and innovation overflows.

Research appears, for instance, that in the force system area, financial specialists' choice to enter a market is fundamentally determined by the apparent danger of defilement. In a comparable style, corruption may bring down the allure of enterprise, occupying innovative ability to less gainful exercises.

This causes shuffling of higher prices and the quality of the products gets down. The OECD report on the outcome of corruption considering the sector level, and further, it prepared the report at the request of the G20. This report shows that the corruption is related to the higher prices for medicines, health services, textbooks, and utility services, among others (OECD, 2015).

An increase in corrupt activities may distort investment, along with the firms which prefer to use their resources for activities which are not productive and are rent-seeking. These activities include lobbying or corruption-specific know-the way so as to be part of the exclusive market of the insiders.

There are companies who prefer to invest in such activities. There are a fewer resources available at such companies for productive investment into either physical or knowledge-based capital. Essentially, corruption is hampering innovation. This effect tends to become even worse, when the trust is lowered because of the corruption in the rule of law, while discouraging the businesses from developing innovations or assets which can further be stolen, extorted, or even expropriated. A report has stated that the possibility of foreign direct investment is approximately 15%. This tends to point lower in countries which show a strong presence of corruption in comparison to the countries that are relatively considered to be free of corruption (Javorcik and Wei, 2009).

6.5.2. Corruption Results in a Waste of Public Resources

Corruption weakens the efficiency and effectiveness of the public sector. Public investments are not offered to the sectors and programs which represent the best money value or where there are high requirements, but for those who offer the best prospects for the personal enrichment of corrupt officials.

OECD research indeed observes that the levels of perceived corruption are high and also, are connected with the lower spending on social services that include health and education, which can reduce the social welfare (OECD, 2015). Biased political decisions may also lead to sector regulations, trade barriers and subsidies that are certainly not in the public interest. Corruption also weakens the quality of civil service.

Where public servants are appointed based on nepotism or favoritism instead of ability and merit, their decisions can put lights on the interests of those who hired them. Besides, the government can be prevented by the corruption from drawing the best talent.

6.5.3. Corruption Deprives the Public Sector of Valuable Revenues

Customs-related corruption can cost an estimated amount of approximately USD 2 billion to World Customs Organization members in customs revenue each year. Similarly, tax evasion can be considered as one of the routes that cause corruption and the fruits of corruption are spilled.

Meanwhile, working on strengthening tax transparency may have positive spill-overs on the fight against corruption, as the two are linked. As countries tend to implement the standard for automatic exchange of financial account information developed by the OECD.

Seeing the change, many countries have also started taking initiative regarding voluntary disclosure programs and other similar initiatives targeted at offshore evasion. This allows taxpayers to regularize' their past tax affairs before they get caught and this can happen when there is increased information sharing. As of now, 30 countries have identified additional revenue totaling over EUR 48 billion considering the past 7 years. Out of which 15 countries, with an estimate 700 000 taxpayers have already come forward under these programs.

6.5.4. Corruption Perpetuates Inequality and Poverty

Corruption is resulting in the rise of inequality in income and well-being. Generally, there have been many countries that have experienced it over the last decade. The inequality can connected with the corruption and the related rent-seeking behavior, misallocation of public funds, and capture of politicians. Inequality of income can also cause inequality in access to political processes and policy discussions.

6.5.5. Corruption Undermines Peace and Democracy

Due to broken democratic systems of checks and balances, media can be easily silenced through bribes from the circumvented rules and regulations. This can cause illicit money flows as well as political crises from weak public budget control.

Corruption has contributed to dirty politics. It tends to influence the elections or the financing of parties and this undermines the rule of the people and thus the very foundation of democracy. The state will eventually lose its credibility and legitimacy if basic public services are not delivered to the citizens due to corruption.

Corruption also increases state exposure to global threats arising from smuggling and illicit trade by organized crime and terrorist groups. A study shows that corruption contributes to terrorism funding and creates inequalities which tend to disenfranchise communities and furthermore, promote the development as well as growth of terrorist groups.

Similarly, illegal financial flows are increasingly connected with the illegal arms trade and also, the drug trafficking. The two of these also play a significant role in the refugee crisis and they tend to facilitate people smuggling.

6.6. DELIMITING POLITICAL CORRUPT

Political corruption is an aspect of illegitimate private gain that defies direct measurement and also, the clear-cut definition. In terms of measurement, researchers have shown confidence in indirect methods and the perceptions of the people.

For private benefit, the public power is misused and this is the most widely used term for corruption which comes under the World Bank's working definition of corruption. TI goes with a much broader term and defines it as the abuse of entrusted and public power for the purpose of private gain.

In this context, the political corruption can be also be defined as abuse of political power for private benefit. But then comes the dilemma of defining what is abuse and what is political During Aristotle, the antiquated Greeks had a comprehension of defilement as a deviation from or depravity of sound government frameworks,

For instance, Tyranny was a corrupted monarchy. Here the monarch no longer contained in mind the well-being of the nation, but he always kept in mind one thing and that is his advantage. Corruption was viewed as a problem of moral decay.

In the 18th century, in England, corruption was considered as encroachment by the executive on the legislature, for instance by money payments, the offer of positions and pensions, and the trading of patronage.

The corruption had violated the principle of authoritarian tendencies, constitutional checks, and balances, and the subsequent decay of the political order. This historical knowledge of corruption concludes two important aspects, namely motives and consequences.

The motive of political corruption is wealth, status, and power, or more particularly self-indulgence, self-enrichment, and power preservation (on contrary to the non-corrupt political leader's concern for the well-being of the nation).

There are several consequences of political corruption which include institutional decay, authoritarian tendencies, arbitrary power, and decreased liberty. However, the consequences of political corruption cannot be considered based on a definition.

That would be like putting the cart in front of the horse. It is not the only factor that the political corruption leads to institutional decay and political oppression. Not all acts of political corruption are even necessary to the detriment of the public interest.'

The corrupt thought process of intensity safeguarding is significant. The worries of the old Greeks acquire the chance of aggregate advantage or increase, notwithstanding private advantage.

Political corruption becomes an integral factor when the rulers or administering elites abuse the assets, they control to support saving their political force. Thus, an increasingly explicit depiction of political corruption would be able to be made.

The most significant aspect of political corruption is that it takes place at the highest levels of the political system. That comes into play at the time of elections where politicians, senior civil servants government ministers, and some other elected, appointed, or nominated senior public officeholders tend to pursue their unfair means.

It happens when these officials, (who make and implement the laws in the name of the people) are themselves corrupt. Moreover, two basic processes are included in the political corruption. The first process takes shape on the demand side of corrupt transactions.

It is the method using which the ruling elites abuse their hold on power for extracting and accumulating the resources. It tends to occur in the case when the political power-holders enrich themselves, individually as well as collectively.

There is the other process and that is the fraudulent conduct of these (and other public) resources for power preservation and also, the expansion. It tends to occur in the case when political power-holders use extracted resources or some other corrupt means for maintaining strengthening their hold on power.

6.6.1. Elements of Political Corruption

Political corruption includes the political decision makers (politicians as well as senior civil servants) who have the power to formulate laws and regulations. Political corruption does not include the civil servants at the implementation end of politics. Also, it does not include the service delivery sectors, despite the fact that the contrast is not clear and bureaucratic corruption can contain a pyramid of upward extraction.

- **Executive Branch:** It includes president, cabinet, and government ministers, top civil servants, including military and security apparatus leaders.
- **Legislative Branch:** It involves members of parliament Judiciary: supreme and high court judges.
- **Local and Regional Authorities:** It includes governors, local

council members, etc. Not included in all definitions.

Political corruption is said to be the way for private gain in illegitimate way by misuse of political power. In particular, it gives the benefits of power, status, and wealth. Most of the political corruption revolves around:

- Status and self-indulgence;
- Maximizing wealth (pecuniary profit);
- Preservation and extension of power;
- Private and collective benefits (individuals, parties, governments).

Usually, the political corruption includes a violation of existing laws and regulations, but it is not restricted to illegal acts. It is also political corruption when national laws and regulations have loopholes and are deliberately neglected, ignored, and even, custom-made. Therefore, the international standards are required to be included while setting a benchmark.

- Breaking of legal statuses and regulatory principles.
- Breaking of international standards and principles.

Political corruption is required to be necessarily included or promise some kind of material inducements, such as money and monetary equivalents like goods and favors.

Political corruption has two basic forms. One of the forms is corrupt accumulation and also, extraction (considering the private sector and national wealth).

This usually happens when politics and business meet together (in the political-private sector nexus, and this is where the corporate money is involved). The other form of the same is a corruption for the preservation and expansion of the power (favoritism and patronage politics). This tends to occur while making political decision and electoral processes.

Corrupt accumulation and extraction include:

- Commissions, bribes, and fees are taken from private sector businesses.
- Undue extraction through customs and taxation.
- Fraud and economic crime.
- Politically created rent-seeking opportunities.
- Politically created market favors benefiting businesses owned by political elites.
- Off-budget transfers manipulated processes of privatization.

- Blackmailing, collecting, and battle financing from the state division, private division and even voters.
- Degenerate methods for power protection incorporate.
- Buying help from political field and some of the dominant parts from different types of collections and government officials.
- Co-optation and support from the benefactor customer systems.
- Buying choices from parliament, legal executive, control, and oversight bodies.
- Preference and support in the designation of government assets.
- Buying voters and votes, discretionary misrepresentation.
- Utilization of open cash for political battles.
- Paying off media and common society.

6.7. DELIMITATIONS IN POLITICAL CIRCLES

6.7.1. Political and Bureaucratic Corruption

The difference between political and bureaucratic corruption is vague because it rather relies on the separation of status of an individual (as a public official) and his/her status (as a private person) and also, the separation of politics from administration.

This qualification is uncertain in most political frameworks. By the by, the qualification has an incredible noteworthiness in expository and down to earth terms. On one hand, political debasement happens at the planning phase of governmental issues, and on the other, bureaucratic, or negligible defilement happens at the usage end of legislative issues.

In this manner, we ought not to consider the qualification of political defilement as the types of debasement that happen in administration conveyance, in social insurance and instruction administrations, and where individuals meet the legislature as customers and clients of open administrations.

The wellbeing would not be worried about normal crooks purchasing out of guardianship, or fixes paid to the open phone organization, or some other type of trivial defilement cases without any political ramifications. Nonetheless, frivolous defilement can once in a while indicate a pyramid of upward extraction. By using this, a little fixes amass into bigger fortunes at the highest point of the framework.

Whether or not neighborhood masters, (for instance, board people and governors) are associated with the thought includes discussion or not. A couple of masters will have them included, others not. We acknowledge this includes a practical framework: a state representative in Nigeria is out and out unique in relation to a close by board of trustees (aggregate) part in Senegal.

6.7.2. Illegal and Immoral

Usually, the political corruption includes the violation of laws and regulations, that exist, by the government officials, but it is not restricted to this. Also, it is said to be the political corruption, when there is a case where there are custom-made loopholes in the national laws and regulations and are deliberately neglected or ignored.

We take an example from President Ferdinand Marcos of the Philippines, who had sections of the Philippines Constitution reformulated to legalize his looting of the nation's wealth. Thus, the dilemma continues about what are the legal, normal, and acceptable political means of influence.

Let us consider the example of the public nominations. There are many presidents who have an exclusive right that he or she can nominate a large number of civil servants of top-level, managers of state companies and parastatals, military, and security personnel, and much more. Obviously, this is the right which should be used politically, for what it is worth for that can be for power preservation, status, and even wealth maximation.

As such, it is observed by many researchers as a major problem (Considering the example of African politics) (excessive presidential), and furthermore, it demonstrates the democratic deficiencies and favoritism. But it is considered as legal within the system provided.

So where is the distinction to be drawn between political corruption and other undue uses of political influence? International standards must be included in setting the benchmarks because political corruption is a breaking of national legal and regulatory principles, and/or breaking of internationally accepted standards and principles.

6.7.3. Money Involved

According to some political scientists, political corruption is termed as a transaction that is held in between the private and public sectors. In this, the collective goods are illegitimately channeled into private pockets. Thus, money enters the definition as a vital aspect. Most of the researchers would argue that some pecuniary benefits must necessarily be included.

Moral and institutional decay is not a vital component in the definition of political corruption, the amassing of material advantages to political leaders. Without the incorporation of cash and material favors in the definition, the idea would contain any kind of illicit as well as ill-conceived political activity (and choice), any type of undue impact, and any maltreatment of political force.

An example can be considered as we take a look back at the Watergate scandal that revealed misuse of political power by the president and his office, to undermine his opponents, in clear violation of the rules in the US. As a result, it resulted in the near impeachment and resignation of President Nixon and also, many of his closest advisors were imprisoned.

However, the Watergate scandal was not political corruption. It was misuse of office, disregarding the constitution, but it was not considered to be corruption. The reason was that it did not involve any pay-offs for any sort of private gain. Money was not the main factor that resulted in the scandalous political decisions.

It is likewise hard to set up the contribution of individual increase or addition for a gathering, for example, the administration or an ideological group, as cash and other material advantages. Particularly testing is guarantees of future advantages, guarantees that can be comprehended all things considered and that can impact choices and loyalties.

A model is the guarantee of future positions, for example, clerical positions given to parliamentarians for sanctioning certain bits of enactment. However, there will be a broad understanding of private as well as group gain which can include issues of favoritism, nepotism, clientelism, and patronage in the definition of political corruption.

6.8. CONCLUSION

The conclusion that can be drawn from the chapter is that we get to know that the bribery is just one form of corruption among many. People, especially the poor, can get hurt when there is wastage of resources. Corruption leads to major loss to the public, and innocent people are not active enough to question them or fight against them. This article about corruption raises a lot of questions some of which are to what degree do the different kinds of corruptions go together? Do all types of corruption originate from the equivalent fundamental causes or do all the different kinds of corruption are caused by different factors? Do the different types of corruption have impact that can be different on society or the political system of the country?

However, this unanswered question continues to persist. As corruption weakens the bone of sustainable economic, political, and social development, for developing, emerging, and developed economies alike. One thing is for sure that we the people are the backbone of the country and its progress is in our hands.

But some people are unable to understand this and so, we do not only let ourselves down but our country too. Because we hold the responsibility for the spreading of corruption, be it at small scale or large the disease continues to spread. In the end, the fourth pillar of our society follows us because the corrupt acts buy the media also, in order to hide the reality to the citizens and this is the situation where it loses its credibility.

REFERENCES

1. Amundsen, I., (2006). *Political Corruption*. [eBook] Available at: https://www.u4.no/publications/political-corruption.pdf (accessed on 25 April 2020).
2. *Definitions of Corruption*, (2014). [eBook] Public Safety Canada. Available at: https://www.publicsafety.gc.ca/cnt/rsrcs/pblctns/rgnzd-crm-brf-48/rgnzd-crm-brf-48-en.pdf (accessed on 25 April 2020).
3. Mind Controversy, (n.d.). *Types of Corruption | With Examples and Related Consequences*. [online] Available at: https://www.mindcontroversy.com/types-corruption-consequences/ (accessed on 25 April 2020).
4. Morris, S., (2011). *Forms of Corruption*. [eBook] Available at: https://www.ifo.de/DocDL/dicereport211-forum2.pdf (accessed on 25 April 2020).
5. n.d. *Putting an End to Corruption*. [eBook] OECD. Available at: https://www.oecd.org/corruption/putting-an-end-to-corruption.pdf (accessed on 25 April 2020).
6. Picci, L., (2019). *Corruption: Conceptualization and Measures*. [online] EUSP. Available at: https://eusp.org/en/news/corruption-conceptualization-and-measures (accessed on 25 April 2020).
7. Šumah, Š., (2018). Corruption, causes, and consequences. *Trade and Global Market*. [online] Available at: https://www.intechopen.com/books/trade-and-global-market/corruption-causes-and-consequences (accessed on 25 April 2020).

Chapter 7

Gender and Politics

CONTENTS

In this chapter, there is a discussion about the conditions of women that face threat of violence while they participate in it or they express their stance politically in many countries. The threat faced by women, and other minorities have been discussed.

In this chapter, the law and violence against woman for involving in politics in Latin American countries and other countries have been discussed. The restrictions of legal reform and need for a broader framework has also been discussed.

In this chapter, there is also discussion of safety of women and need for law to protect them against violence they faced politically. The limit of legal reform has also been discussed in this chapter.

The growth of the feminist movement with the theme of nationalism has alarmed the political and social scientists has also been discussed in this chapter.

7.1. INTRODUCTION

Politics as a phenomenon of the real world and political science as a subject in academics are being gendered. The people around the world consider that their basic living conditions their security, health, education, employment, as well as reach to market, public space, and free expression are profoundly influenced by their identity as belonging to specific sex or gender categories.

The individual bodies can be coded as male or female, heterosexual or homosexual, transgendered, or nongendered in a number of various forms across cultures and over time. However, in the social contexts in which they occur these gender social practices often appear natural and unproblematic, even biological and therefore impossible to change.

Yet, considering the wide variety of the number and substance of gender categories across social contexts, a cursory review of the literature on the biological basis of sex shows a world far more dynamic than this simplistic male-female dichotomy would indicate (Butler, 1990; Dreger, 1998; Fausto-Sterling, 2000).

The Gender is never just about sex, but varies according to race, ethnicity, nation, class, and a variety of other social dimensions.

Even so, the pervasive, dichotomous sex-typing feature of many modern world organizations would be a matter of intellectual curiosity if the implications of identifying with a particular gender were not so dire. The Gender around the globe dictates who goes hungry and gets adequate nutrition and water, who can vote, run for office, marry or have rights to children, who controls power and respect and who is denigrated and discarded, and one that is most vulnerable to violence and abuse in their own homes and intimate relationships (Htun, 2003; Htun and Weldon, 2011).

Such norms form more than personal and family relationships or career paths, while they undoubtedly shape the following: they shape religious practice and market structure and governance processes (Charrad, 2010; Brettell and Sargeant, 2001; Lamphere, 2001).

Let's consider just a few concrete examples. When one look at some of the main issues that make up the partisan divide between political parties in the United States whether reproductive rights or same-sex marriage they can see that many of the issues surrounding culture wars are essentially questions about which male and female sexual and interpersonal practices should be tolerated and embraced by society at large (Wolbrecht, 2000; Inglehart and Norris, 2003; Sanbonmatsu, 2002).

In the Philippines, income from domestic worker care job is the number one export and the main source of foreign currency, while Lim in 1998 stated that sex work income accounts for between 2 and 11% of Thailand's gross domestic product.

As well as finally, the global economic crisis has had a much differentiated impact since 2008 in terms of the resulting cuts in spending and austerity programs.

It is clear that some groups are much more adversely affected than others, and many women that make up a large proportion of state and public-sector employees, and the majority of single parents and the poor have been particularly hard hit and affected differently from men (Waylen, 2012).

Most deeply perhaps, gender affects the very ways in which we organize and think about the world and our way of knowing the world.

In such an environment, it is hardly shocking that these social norms on sex and sexuality often define political science as a discipline and fundamentally form it. The study of politics, as we will see, has now expanded beyond the narrow focus on those holding formal office and distribution politics.

It now includes many new groups supporting gender trouble as well as new ideas about masculinity and femininity across a variety of contexts, from home to Parliament houses. And despite the vibrancy of the gender and political scholarship shown in this handbook and a long history of gender advocacy, in much academic political science gender is still overlooked (Figure 7.1).

Figure 7.1: Women protesting against violence they face for participating in politics.

Sources: Image by Wikimedia.

7.2. AN INCOMPLETE REVOLUTION

The starting point is to acknowledge the tremendous changes that have taken place as a discipline over the last century, both in politics as practice and in political science. They do not subscribe to a traditional metanarrative, often seen in political science and other disciplines, of a predominantly patriarchal world that started to evolve as feminism spread to the rest of the world portrayed as originating in the West in the 1960s.

It is noteworthy, however, that in 1950 the vast majority of the world's legislators were male and that, in most cases, family law had favored men in areas ranging from property rights that include inheritance rights and children's rights to sexual rights (Interparliamentary Union (IPU); Htun and Weldon, 2011) male supremacy in formal, decision-making roles seemed normal and uncontestable, and male authority in the family was seen as a biological necessity and mark of civilization since colonial times.

Such trends of male domination have inevitably been contextualized and challenged by feminist activists and academics, pointing out that male domination are neither inevitable nor desirable. Anthropologists have recorded the wide range of family structures and social organizational modes around the world, questioning any attempt to theorize a universal public-private split or male dominance model (Lamphere, 2001).

For example, the trading in market was seen as exclusive domain of women in Indonesia (Brenner, 2001). And in North America, the Oneida (a community of First Nations) traditionally viewed organized politics (taking collective decisions) as the domain of women (Sunseri, 2011). Thus, the exclusion of women from the public sphere described as leadership positions in community decision-making and economic affairs cannot be viewed as continuous throughout history or as universal.

The studies also show that the notion of the apparently universal patriarchal family structure is bankrupt. Historical and current types of the family vary widely from polyandry that is one wife, many husbands to polygyny that is one husband, many wives and include matrifocal and matrilineal structures where inheritance and parentage systems move through women (Menon, 2001).

None of these organizational types necessarily preclude male dominance, but they warn us against universalizing public and private stories and rising gender roles. Thus, the notion that until the 1970s the planet was dominated by a hierarchical patriarchal structure does not bear the anthropological or historical background (Brettell and Sargeant, 2001; Jolly and Macintyre, 1989).

Nor is it right that feminism should be seen as a Western innovation or a recent concept. As Jayawardena in 1986 stated, Debates on women's rights and education took place in China in the 18th century, and campaigns for women's social liberation took place in India in the early 19th century;

feminist struggles emerged in many Asian countries between 60 and 80 years ago.

The fact that such movements occurred in several non-European countries during this time was hidden from history. Enlightenment thinkers like Mary Wollstonecraft and John Stuart Mill argued in favor of women's liberation, with Wollstonecraft writing A Vindication of Women's Rights as early as 1792 and Mill the Women's Subjection in 1789.

Nevertheless, as a result of women's activism over the last century, they have seen dramatic changes in attitudes towards sexuality and gender in every region of the world, as well as a transformation of laws and policies on a wide range of issues, including violence against women (VAW), family law, women's access to political power and education, the criminalization of homosexuality, and maternity and parental leave. Though these changes have by no means been uniform or uncontested (Weldon, 2002; Htun, 2003; Krook, 2009; Charrad, 2010; Htun and Weldon, 2011).

In nearly every country in the world, women have mobilized to claim their rights, though with varying degrees of success (Htun and Weldon, 2012). Feminist activists have used a wide range of strategies to claim certain rights, from street theater to petitions and lobbying.

The number of women in Europe, Asia, and Latin America that are prominent politicians and heads of state and international bodies has increased. Since 1980, women have been in excess of 30 national leaders.

Hillary Clinton has been the U.S. Secretary of State in this decade alone (the sixth woman to hold the post in the last three administrations), and Michele Bachelet, Cristina Fernandez de Kirchner, and Dilma Roussef have been elected presidents in Chile, Argentina, and Brazil, respectively.

Ellen Johnson Sirleaf was elected as Liberia's president, and in 2011, Christine Lagarde became the first female director of the International Monetary Fund (IMF).

The parity cabinet of the socialist government of Zapatero in Spain (2004 to 2008) contained equal numbers of male and female ministers and outraged the defense establishment with the appointment of a visibly pregnant woman as minister of defense (Waylen, 2012). And in November 2011, Rwanda, and Andorra's lower government houses were made up of at least 50% women.

The field of political science has also been changed too. There are more women at present that are taking part in academic politics research. In 2002, women constitute 35% of assistant professors in the United States (APSA, 2004).

There were also some very prominent and influential female political scientists. The political scientist Elinor Ostrom became the first woman to win the Nobel Prize for Economics in 2009.

And lately, the academy as a whole has made several significant efforts to create more equal conditions for women. It would therefore be impossible to deny that substantial efforts and accomplishments have been made, both in terms of increasing the political representation of women and in terms of improving the opportunities for women scholars in the academy in general (Waylen, 2012).

But both the society and the disciplines are still dominated today by men. In November 2011, the global average for women in the lower house of legislatures was still only 20%, a statistic that conceals some large variations ranging from an average of 42.3% in the Nordic Countries to 12.9% in the Pacific region (Inter-Parliamentary Union).

Only 6 of 37 Under-Secretary-Generals at the United Nations that is 16% were women. Yet international business perhaps remains the most male-dominated of those areas of power; and women make up just 1.4% of Fortune 500 corporations 'chief executives.

Women also struggle on a day-to-day basis to change their living conditions. Every minute a woman dies in childbirth, and in the third world, 99% of these maternal deaths occur.

Women constitute a majority of the poor in the world and are disproportionately illiterate. The revolution in science is still incomplete, with only 22% of female political scientists in the United States and the United Kingdom in 2002 and fewer women in the highest ranks and the most prestigious universities in study (APSA, 2004).

Gender and political theorists argue that the origins of this continuing male domination are complex and deep in both society and the academy of political science.

Challenging this deep-seated dominance is more than just a matter of adding women to the public office or the sheer numbers (Beckwith and Cowell-Meyers, 2003). It's not enough in itself though significant. In order to make them gender-equitable, the more major change is needed both to politics as a practice and to political science as a discipline. To encourage this, they need to understand what it is about politics as an academic discipline and politics as a culture and the ways the two connect that contribute to this over-representation of men and a profound ignorance of gender.

When one first considers the nature of politics and political science as an academic discipline, there are several interconnected factors that jump out. Firstly, as Virginia Sapiro in 1981 has stated, part of the reason for the gender blindness of the discipline lies in the low number of women in the discipline.

For her, the women's institutional status reproduces the discipline's androcentric assumptions. Second, and perhaps more critically, privileged men have established the definitions and methods of the discipline to identify certain things that are of interest to them.

This supremacy is reflected in the very narrow and political conceptions of what counts as a politics historically focused on by the Anglo-American disciplines. Politics, loosely built, is the political or governing operation.

Yes, Aristotle used the word politics in the original Greek to connote all queries pertaining to the operation of polis, the political class. Politics is characterized by its public or general nature, the way in which it affects the community as a whole, as distinct from private matters (Arendt, 1958; Wolin, 1960).

Politics, too, is seen as the study of strength, and sometimes the study of the strong by definition. But some wider concepts of politics have also had a long history in political science.

Dahl in 1984 stated politics as related to power and political structures as any continuous pattern of human relationships that involves control, influence, power or authority to a significant extent. Others link politics fundamentally with distributions, such as who gets what, where, when, and how the authoritative allocation of value (Easton, 1953).

The traditional emphasis on politics as the study of governmental and electoral machinery or political elites and formal institutions made women and gender invisible despite their fundamental importance in building the welfare state and building post-colonial nations, in conducting war and terrorism, and in preserving more general social and economic privilege.

The origins of these core assumptions about what constitutes politics can be traced in the Anglo-American tradition to the work of political theorists like John Locke, who based many of their theories on the theoretical distinction of the public and the private spheres (Figure 7.2).

Figure 7.2: Woman protesting against ban on abortion in Latin America.

Sources: Image by Wikipedia.

7.3. THE LAW AND VIOLENCE AGAINST WOMEN (VAW) IN POLITICS

7.3.1. VAWIP Legally Defined

The Bolivian Association of Local Councilors and Mayors (ACOBOL) drafted Law 243. The first data and testimony of victims of VAWIP were gathered by this group. ACOBOL realized through this process that women politicians are in a legal limbo.

The Current electoral laws and legislation on VAW that could be used to protect them were insufficient because many of their actions, like the denial of wages, were not included in those laws. This is also the case in other countries in the region and explains why activists seeking to combat VAWIP prefer the legislative path. Legal definitions are important for assessment of VAWIP because they draw boundary lines around the phenomenon; determine what it is and what it is not. Law 243 differentiates between political harassment and political violence.

Harassment is characterized as an act of pressure, intimidation, harassment or threats by a person or group of persons, whether directly or through a third party, against women candidates, elected, and appointed officials, or those performing a public service, or against their families, for the purpose of shortening or suspending impeding or restricting the functions attached to her post.

Political violence is defined in a similar framework as physical, psychological, or sexual actions, behaviors, and or aggressions (Asamblea Legislativa Plurinacional, 2012, Art. 7a, 7b).

Differentiating between harassment and violence presumes that harm is not caused by harassment, though it is caused by the violence. Interviews, therefore, indicate that this separation was a strategic move by activists that viewed the distinction between harassment and violence as a matter of degree rather than type.

As a result of this distinction, violence, and harassment were legally defined as separate phenomena with different sanctions, although there is still some slippage in use as in Article 8 of Law 243 that replicates the act of political harassment and violence. These definitions have reappeared in legislative proposals in other countries in Latin America, albeit with a few additions or omissions.

For example, the Ecuadorean bill includes verbal violence, whereas the Mexican electoral authorities Protocol for Responding to Political Violence considers economic violence (TEPJF, 2016). Often, these bills differ with respect to the sanctions imposed and the measures developed to avoid VAWIP.

7.3.2. Limits to Legal Definitions

In spite of the advantages of typifying VAWIP and sanctioning specific behaviors, legal definitions only provide a partial perspective on the way victims experience VAWIP and what it really is. One issue with legal definitions is that they describe harassment and violence as a sequence of discrete actions, rather than as part and parcel of the same issue. Therefore, this ignores the fact that, in most cases, various VAWIP manifestations take place simultaneously with the same patient and over long periods of time (Escalante and Mendez, 2011; Herrera, Arias, and Garcia, 2012; Quintanilla, 2012).

At the time of analyzing some of the cases, the interconnection between different manifestations of VAWIP becomes evident. Maybe VAWIP's most emblematic case is that of Juana Quispe, a Bolivian local councilor. Quispe was wrongly accused of corruption after being elected and compelled to resign by the mayor and other members of the city council.

She denied the accusations, refusing to give up her seat, after which the council unlawfully disqualified her (Corz, 2012; Pando, 2016). She was returned to her seat after a long legal battle but was refused the salary she was owed, on the grounds of the fact that she had not attended council meetings during this period. Thirty-two days after her return, and only a few days before she was due to give testimony against the mayor, she was assassinated.

In spite of all the evidence indicating the crime was politically motivated, police ruled it a robbery and the perpetrators were never prosecuted. Clearly, this case shows that VAWIP cannot be reduced to a single move. It also points to the limitations of making a clear distinction between violence and harassment.

According to the statute, only Quispe's assassination was considered an act of aggression but she had been regularly abused, humiliated, and threatened prior to her assassination, and her property was damaged (Pando, 2016).

All these acts served the same purpose: pressuring her to leave her seat so that she could take her place as her replacement. Instead of being unrelated events, as the law implies, looking at all these events as part of the same pattern as VAWIP shows not only the nature of her pain, but also the perpetrators intent and motives. In addition, this case shows that VAWIP is both an example of VAW, and an attempt at democratic values and electoral institutions.

7.3.3. A Broader Framework

The assessment by Feminist of VAW are crucial when it comes to understanding the way VAWIP affects those that suffer it, as well as the way they can better understand it.

Rather than assessing the VAW as distinct actions, feminist scholars describe VAW as a continuum of actions that contain a wide range of behaviors (Marin and Felipe Russo, 1999), on the grounds that all of these behaviors affect the self-worth, emotional well-being, and mental health of the victim (Connors and Harway, 1995; DeKeseredy, 2011; Kilpatrick, 2004).

In many other cases, VAW victims suffer concurrently from several types of abuse including economic control, psychological or physical assault, harassment, bullying, intimidation, and stalking.

These behaviors are not mutually exclusive and are not experienced as separate occurrences but rather as being closely linked (DeKeseredy, 2011). Accordingly, thc wcight of multiple harms is borne by the same person, giving the abuse a cumulative effect much greater than the mere sum of its parts (Stark, 2007).

Therefore, harassment and abuse even if they do not culminate in physical harm are part of the same phenomenon and should therefore be conceptualized as such. Using definitions based on gradations means certain actions are worse or more harmful than others.

While certain VAWIP crimes, such as abduction, rape, or assassination, are undeniably worse than assault, these acts are severe and are typically accompanied by subtler actions not generally viewed as aggression.

Paying enough attention to subtler forms of violence can prevent the most extreme forms, since these signals are taken seriously as acts of violence in all their forms. Simultaneously, many women view such seemingly harmless actions as worse than physical violence (Follingstad, 1990; Stark, 2007).

Ultimately, these different forms have the same purpose: to reinforce power structures and to convey a secondary status to women (Connors and Harway, 1995).

Looking at VAWIP in a more systematic way accounts not only for its effects on victims and their families but also for its impact on political institutions and democratic values. VAWIP should be known not only in terms of the impact it has on the individual but also in terms of its impacts on political processes and democratic values.

The Leidig has already stated that it can be difficult to identify the severity of any specific form of violence. Certainly, any measure of the toxicity of a victimization act must consider both its wider social implications and the victim's life circumstances.

By forcing women out of office, VAWIP perpetrators not only send a message that women are not welcome but also undermine gender equality legislation. They also disregard electoral procedures by denying voters the right of the person they choose to be represented.

More generally, they show disdain for democratic values by denying all people, men, and women alike, the right to participate in the decisions that affect them (Figure 7.3).

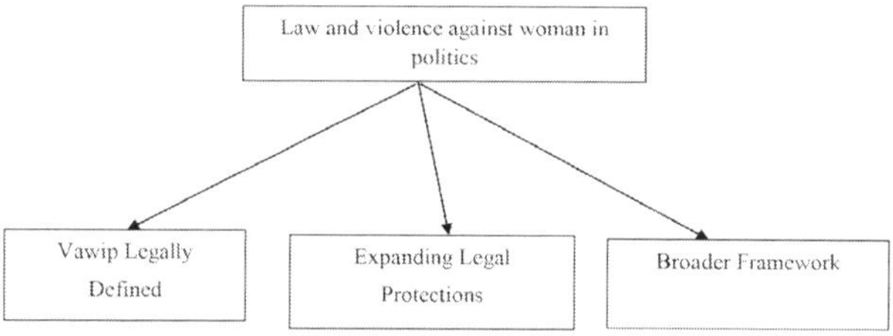

Figure 7.3: The law and violence against woman in politics.

7.4. FIGHTING VIOLENCE AGAINST WOMAN IN POLITICS

The new Inter-Parliamentary Union survey of female parliamentarians highlights the global dimensions of a troubling trend that in 39 nations, 44% of women surveyed reported receiving murder, rape, abuse, or abduction threats. One fifth said they were victims of sexual violence.

The murder of British Labor MP Jo Cox, who in June 2016 was fatally shot and stabbed outside a library in her district, brought public attention to the violent online threats that British female politicians face on daily basis threats that the media and the public have often dismissed as irrelevant.

In politics, VAW is not a new phenomenon. Women seeking political power have always faced opposition.

However, as more and more women are running for office around the world, citing their right to equal representation as enshrined in the UN CEDAW Convention, the opposition has escalated and become more apparent. Over the past two decades, in a framework of structural inequality, dozens of countries have implemented legislative quotas and parity laws to ensure women's political representation. While the shortcomings of such measures have been highly debated, it is clear that they have allowed more women to enter politics than ever before. However, efforts to promote women's political leadership have seldom been combined with strategies for ensuring their public safety and well-being. Political systems are often patriarchal institutions, resistant to reform, and aggressive when questioned, as the feminist scholars have long argued.

The Politicians of all sexes inevitably face threats and intimidation, especially in countries where violence is ingrained in the logic of political competition. Yet existing research shows women candidates and politicians are faced with specific risks. They are often targeted because of their status as women and targeted in gender-specific ways.

For example, female politicians especially those who stand in the way of male opponents or powerful interest groups are routinely threatened with rape, harassed with sexist remarks, or accused of sexual and moral impurity.

Threats and harassment often come from multiple sides: opposition parties and supporters but also from colleagues and communities related to women. Women that enter politics in many cultures often face threats and restrictions within the private sphere.

7.4.1. Expanding Legal Protections

Violence and abuse hinder fair involvement in politics by woman by preventing them from running for office, damaging their political prospects, or pressuring them to ally with powerful male figures for defense, or otherwise compromising their policy agenda.

But in many ways, female politicians' threats and abuse are ignored as trivial just online rant, imaginary not about gender, or routine just the expense of doing politics. Violence offenders seldom are brought to justice.

The Supporters in a number of countries have pushed for legal reforms in response to these different forms of silencing that would formally recognize the specific threats women face in politics and close existing gaps in protection.

These types of efforts took various forms. Some lobbied to expand existing laws that prohibit gender-based discrimination in the workplace or VAW generally. Others have promoted new legislation to codify VAW as a separate and unique crime in politics.

Across Latin America, where VAW across politics is a constant problem, the drive for criminalization has been most important. In 2016, the Regional Conference on Women in Latin America and the Caribbean at ECLAC described political harassment as a primary barrier to women's political participation across the region.

Though Bolivia remains the only country to date to have passed a law specifically prohibiting and criminalizing VAW in politics (Law 243 of May 2012), at least five other countries have been debating similar bills.

The Bolivian law was the result of tireless lobbying by the Bolivian Association of Councilors (ACOBOL) and its allies, as they recorded thousands of political harassment incidents around the country especially in rural areas.

The law aims at both harassment and physical and psychological violence, provides detailed descriptions of the acts under its jurisdiction, and establishes specific administrative, penal, and constitutional sanctions. Over the past several years, Bolivian experience has encouraged activists and parliamentarians around the world to press for similar legislative changes.

Throughout Peru, Ecuador, El Salvador, Mexico, and Costa Rica, several draft laws have been proposed throughout parliament but have yet to be implemented.

Parliamentarians frequently refer to existing legislation that does not govern VAW legislators. In Peru, for example, the National Plan against Gender Violence 2016–2021 first acknowledged political harassment as a particular form of gender-based violence, but a bill aimed at criminalization remains stalled in parliament.

In Mexico, proposals to bring more concrete measures to address VAW in politics into pre-existing electoral and gender-based discrimination laws have been adopted by the Senate, but a new protocol has been introduced to combat political VAW but has yet to be enforced.

Amid these difficulties, Bolivian legislation and parallel legal reform efforts have been instrumental in drawing attention to the high levels of violence and harassment faced by women politicians across the country. Activists have used legislative proposals as a method to illustrate the flaws in existing legal systems and advocate for more to be done by political parties and election bodies.

As feminist legal scholar Catherine MacKinnon argues, laws that label a particular occurrence and criminalize it can help legitimize accidents as injuries and delegitimize our victimization by them. Considering that VAW in politics is very often aimed at silencing and erasing the goals, it should not underestimate the power of legal recognition.

Laws may help raise public awareness and question the idea that acts of violence are merely the cost of politics. Law 243 has provided a significant platform for mobilization and activism by the civil society in Bolivia.

Five years after its adoption, however, it is clear that the legislation still suffers from significant weaknesses. It does not provide safeguards to protect the person reporting violence events from possible reprisals, fails to take into account the unique vulnerabilities of indigenous women, and fails to cover women who are involved in social organizations regardless of the fact that the latter also serves as women's entry point into political life.

Moreover, by far the biggest challenge arises from poor implementation and enforcement a weakness that underlines the limits of legislative approaches to women-violence in politics.

7.4.2. The Limits of Legal Reform

ACOBOL has registered hundreds of acts of harassment and violence against Bolivian women politicians since 2012. In 2016, only one resulted in a conviction and the reinstatement of a council woman forced to resign her seat. Police continue to relate VAW in politics to general fear rather than gender-specific discrimination.

Furthermore, the adjudication processes do not guarantee timely access to justice, which means that victims often stay in limbo for months, if not years, while their case goes through the system. These difficulties illustrate the drawbacks of legal reform in the sense of general insecurity and injustice.

First because of their gender identity and other forms of political violence, it can be difficult to distinguish between violence directed towards women especially since the latter can still manifest and are experienced in gendered ways.

The structurally inferior position of women influences how they perceive the violent or oppressive practices already embedded within the social fabric. A narrow focus on criminalization can neglect the greater systemic and cultural forces that undermine democratic competition, as well as their particular and often overwhelmingly negative impact on women.

Second, while legislation can help mobilize public opinion and change societal attitudes, effective enforcement mechanisms often rely on it. When justice systems are sluggish and unreliable, and police forces provide sources of risk rather than defense, legal changes that put the burden on institutions for criminal justice are likely to offer little redress.

In a study of gender-based violence laws in El Salvador, Walsh, and Menjivar found that despite the existence of legal protections, judicial officials frequently view VAW as usual in a context of generalized insecurity especially VAW who are already oppressed in terms of race, ethnicity, or social class.

The Inaction on the part of the justice system means that criminalized violence tends to be normalized: victims are forced to compromise with aggressors, or their cases are dismissed.

Ultimately, legal codifications are inherently limited and do not necessarily reflect sufficiently the perceptions of harm experienced by women. They usually give weight to physical injury and are traditionally not well-equipped to handle the broader scope of political, cultural, or psychological violence.

Even the Bolivian Law 243, drafted in close collaboration with feminist activists, conceives VAW in politics as a series of distinct harmful acts, while not actually considering the way various forms of discrimination, marginalization, and harassment can intersect and intensify each other over time. The multidimensional nature of the issue requires holistic approaches, tailored to the political context.

VAW politicians in many countries are at the crossroads of different social and political challenges, the institutionalized sexism, and traditional gender norms, high levels of impunity and weak rule of law, and the normalization of everyday political and criminal violence.

Ensuring full political participation by women in these contexts requires addressing these challenges in parallel while paying attention to the connections between them is surely no easy task.

Across existing democracies, the emphasis focuses largely on combating online and offline violence, while questioning the wider sexist assumptions and systemic obstacles that continue to undermine women's political progress. The thing that binds these contexts is the need to address the underlying culture of entitlement that allows for brushing aside violence and harassment. Therefore, better data collection and ongoing awareness rising are key priorities, as are efforts to establish strict codes of conduct and accountability mechanisms within parliament and political parties. To make gains in political representation sustainable, taking women's experiences seriously and advancing protection strategies and initiatives to fight back against the inevitable backlash is crucial.

7.5. GENDER NORMS AND WOMEN'S POLITICAL PARTICIPATION: GLOBAL TRENDS AND FINDINGS ON NORM CHANGE

The year 2018 is marked as a year of political participation by women. Last Spring, 113 women in Lebanon registered as candidates for parliament, an eight-fold increase since 2009. With the highest number of women parliamentarians in the world, Rwanda broke records, the lower house containing more women than men that is 63.8%. The pink wave of 100 women in the US set a record for female representation at the congress.

And yet, political representation of women on a global level remains limited even unequal. UN data shows that, in 2016, just 22.8% of all national parliamentarians were women that are up from 11.3% in 1995. Only eleven women serve as heads of state. And the UN itself, and many of its departments, remain largely headed by men.

Which determines unequal political representation is a complex matter. But to facilitate more inclusive political systems, a greater understanding of negative gender norms and norm-change approaches is necessary.

7.5.1. Voting Politics and Gender Norms

The role of women in politics as candidates, delegates, fundraisers, and group mobilizers is influenced in different ways by gender norms.

As argued by Ronald Inglehart and Pippa Norris, perceptions of appropriate gender roles in politics are formed by wider trends of social values and priorities, which in turn rely on economic development and religious traditions. In this way, more economically developed and secular democracies are correlated with more balanced attitudes towards gender.

The ability of women to have their voices heard as voters, in its simplest form, has long been shaped by gender norms in addition to other factors such as wealth, race, and ethnicity. For instance, prevailing norms about women's family responsibilities have denied them their fundamental voting rights for centuries worldwide.

Culture reform, expressed in today's complete formal global empowerment of women in every country holding elections except the Vatican, with Saudi Arabia granting women the vote most recently in 2015, has strengthened women's voices in politics.

Within today's democracies, there are also gender differences within voter conduct and engagement. While women are excluded from voting in some contexts (such as certain areas in Pakistan), men and women tend to vote at about the same rate in most democracies, a trend attributed to greater gender equality in education and participation in the workforce.

But women are still lagging behind in global political participation such as contributing to elections, joining political organizations, or contacting officials. The explanations include norms on gender roles that can eat up their time, as well as income gaps, civic skills and education, and relations with groups such as trade unions.

Though this is evolving. For instance, in the US, women, and men vote equally and are equally likely to take part in a protest or sign a petition. Women are more likely to sign a petition or raise money for a political cause in a survey spanning 18 western democracies yet are less likely to join a protest.

7.5.2. Women's Movements and Gender Norms

The willingness of women to participate politically both inside and outside the voting booth especially as community organizers and elected officials is often influenced by expectations that drive broader social structures.

There is a major fact to face women carry a triple burden of economic, successful and community work. It, in effect, is influenced by gendered social norms that raise perceptions about women's roles and affect the willingness of women to run for office and participate in politics.

They also know that in defending traditional gender norms, some women use political activism. For instance, in Japan, Kimiko Osawa's 2015 study of anti-feminist conservative women in Japan highlighted that some engage in political activism without betraying their commitment to traditional domestic roles, in their view.

Moreover, Miki Caul Kittilson found that while in Western Europe women tend to support leftist parties, in post-communist countries they tend to favor the right. Recent data on that women's participation in far-right parties across Europe show that their engagement does not always support feminist representation or policies.

The entrenched ideas about women's roles can mobilize political movements, sometimes with the backing of women that aim to further strengthen them. As Deniz Kandioyti's Turkey research notes states gender concepts have become a central pillar of populism and maintaining, the existing gender order has been crucial to nationalist politics.

Women's political participation in unstable and conflict-affected countries is also a major priority. Although there is a growing focus on the role of women, including in the recent UN Security Council, recent CARE research under Every Voice Counts initiative finds that women in most conflict settings are still excluded from formal political processes.

Although women have played a key role in resolving violence in South Sudan and Sierra Leone for example, they continue to be invisible in subsequent peace-building and political processes. It confirms work by Georgina Waylen and others who argue that although women's movements have helped to overthrow many authoritarian regimes, they have had less representational impact once democracy is implemented.

As Waylen's work on Latin America demonstrates, women's participation in issues of' high' and' grassroots' politics is crucial for more sustainable political representation and equality, both inside and outside the state and party systems.

7.5.3. Political Representation and Gender Norms

A further key issue is representation. Gender norms weaken the role of women in public life, causing opposition to political leadership by women. The traditions that keep women out of politics often form the way people vote and how women will spend their time and behave, placing practical limits on public and political participation.

Debates on women's representation in political leadership and organizations-the who versus the is portrayed, and the politics of ideas versus the politics of presence remain essential to our understanding of the way to achieve gender equality in politics.

In spite of the quota fever of the 1990, and the introduction of gender quota schemes to elect more female officials, legislative gender quotas are still being contested and their enforcement is still a challenge.

Moreover, research suggests that women do not necessarily vote women over men on the basis of politics of gender identity, but instead their views and priorities are central. Though women generally support leftist parties in Western Europe, they also tend to favor the right in Post-Communist countries, implying that women's voting blocs are not monolithic.

However, research shows that the more closely a government represents society as a whole, the more stable and peaceful it is likely that government will be. Similarly, some data suggest that women are more likely to address policies that affect women than men, even those without a feminist agenda, even though the data is kept somewhat equivocal in this area and there are exceptions, and more research is needed.

7.5.4. Politics, Gender Norms and Young People: Looking Ahead

It takes time to change norms, so one can one fosters more equitable political systems. Young people should be a significant focal point. Research has found that young women are less likely to participate in party politics than young men worldwide in societies influenced by negative gender norms.

Sustainable gender equality demands strong youth role models. For example, in India researchers found that men in certain areas who were exposed to at least two female village leaders were more likely to vote for women in general.

To young women it's also crucial to see themselves in leadership positions. They encourage younger women to take similar social risks like political participation as groundbreaking women crack expectations and stereotypes.

The drive is being led by a number of initiatives to involve young women in civic education and training from Running Start in Washington D.C., to CEPWOP in Nigeria, to Aware Girls in Pakistan. They directly target women and girls in civic education and leadership training to promote better participation and involvement of women in government and politics.

Other initiatives like the FRIDA Young Feminist Fund support grassroots women's groups and movements to allow for greater mobilization. Certain leadership skills initiatives like Rise Up and its Let Girls Lead campaign emphasize the leadership skills and knowledge of girl's rights.

In addition to role models and greater study and activism, they need a mix of such efforts to push ahead for more inclusive, stable, and sustainable global political structures.

7.6. THE DISTURBING RISE OF FEMONATIONALISM

In the fall of 2018, Nicole Hochst, a member of the nationalist Alternative for Germany (AFD) group, during an interview with Der Spiegel said she was worried about Germany's future and the protection of women from radical Islamists and migrants.

Alice Weidel, a lesbian leader of the political party, alleged that the lack of protection for women and girls has resulted in increased migration into Germany. Through expressing their support for gender equality in sexist, xenophobic words, they provide catering for a subset of women mainly, anti-migrant, and anti-Islamic ethnic Germans that are willing to join the AFD.

Their goal is to build a broader base for advocating pronationalist policies for ethnic Germans, alleging Muslims as a danger to women, and calling for more criminalization of non-German migrants.

She stated that she believes that they are the only party in Germany that is really fighting for women's rights, because they point out that they are in danger of losing the freedoms and rights of women for which they have been fighting for centuries, Hochst said, referring to state-sanctioned programs for mothers, pay equity and more public safety in Germany.

This strategy of using the rights of women, interventionist nationalistic policies and the language of feminism for far-right purposes is not uncommon. European conservatives, secularists, and right-wing politicians have usurped women's rights and feminism to infringe religious freedom, women's bodies and migration under the umbrella that feminist theorist Sara Farris terms femonationalism.

In the early 2000s, a number of Western European countries adopted laws to criminalize refugees or Muslim women simultaneously. The Italians passed Law No. 177 in July 2002 that required fingerprinting of migrants and imposed severe sanctions on undocumented migrants.

In France, the 2004 ban on headscarf in public schools resulted in the government's desire to see Muslim women accept the concept of laicité (secularism) in France.

These legal structures are some of the many iterations of the way European politics has become more dominant in an ideological formation built on an anti-migrant and anti-Muslim foundation.

Femonationalism is also a wellspring for white nationalism, with people like feminist Susan Moller Okin claiming that women are more oppressive to non-Western cultures.

Unlike Moller Okin, Rita Chin argues that the crisis of multiculturalism is not a result of refugees or ethnic minorities harmful to Western society;

rather, it is a product of enduring legacies of racial nationalism in the 19th century and stagnant conceptions of what it means to be European white, Christian, and secular.

At the heart of these anxieties is what Joan Wallach Scott defines as the perspective of Western liberal democracies through a racist lens that had justified imperial conquest and viewed mostly Muslim people not just as different but as inferior. This has been going on for some time.

British colonialists in India, as scholar Gayatri Spivak observed, justified colonialism because they saw themselves as saving brown women from brown men which is percolating from nationalist and far-right groups in Europe today.

In the scope of European racism, how one can explain those racialized comments. And why it is essential to talk about this movement now.

At a time when racist, antisemitic, and Islamophobic attacks are on the rise, it is important to focus on how feminist language is used to fulfilling the goal of right-wing populism to criminalize migrants, dictate what Muslim women should wear, and deviate from existing sexist policies in European society.

As this brand of populism has exploded in recent years, it has sought to rebrand itself across Europe to cater to a new generation of voters, especially with Marine Le Pen minimally distancing itself from the campaign of her father by welcoming more women and gay people into the Front National Party.

The emergence of far-right parties has created a litany of self-described feminists who come from Scandinavia to Southern Europe to suggest nationalist cordon.

The Parties like the Swedish Democrats, the Swiss People's Party and the AFD, adhering to national conservatism, jettison themselves from centrist parties by championing their burgeoning female members. They expect to do what their predecessors don't have that is attaining gender parity in leadership.

European nationalist parties have had women's caucuses developed. For example, with the introduction of the Frauen in der Alternative, a working group that aims to increase female voters in their party structure, AFD has tried to appeal to women under the leadership of Alice Weidel and Beatrix von Storch. Some of the AFD members went so far as to fight through the language of the Me-Too movement for women's rights. And many non-white women are held in contempt; their position is enshrined in anti-Islamic rhetoric that then reproduces anti-feminist policies both tied to productive and reproductive forces in society.

AFD leader Dennis Augustin proclaimed Islam was not compatible with our liberal-democratic constitution and Islam is totalitarian. The party goes even further by stating Muslims refuse to integrate, that harps over the ways in which Islamic religiosity could be expressed. Simultaneously, a recent article revealed that Weidel, a prominent Party leader, hired an asylum seeker to clean her home.

European political leaders frequently make migrant and Muslim women scapegoats without addressing the ways in which racism is engendered in their own socicty.

While Elisa Banfi has mentioned, countries like Switzerland have traditionally introduced burqa bans in the name of women's rights, even though gender parity has not been fully achieved in electoral politics. Although Switzerland today functions as a direct democracy, women make up only 30% of its representative house and 15% of the senate.

Instead of addressing the uneven political representation and power of women across the continent, a demand that could also address the ongoing global gender gap law has been fixed on Muslim women's apparel.

One German court prohibited a Muslim teacher from wearing headscarf, leaving her temporarily unemployed and being reassigned for work to another institution. The anti-hijab debate in France is a phenomenon which is constantly evolving and mutating.

The country banned the wearing full-face veils in 2010. The various French politicians in 2016 tried to ban Muslim women from wearing swimsuits covering their entire bodies widely known as burkinis.

As European states use laws to restrict women's access to education, job opportunities, and leisure activities that decide to wear the hijab, veil, or burka, they impede these women from having control over their labor and body autonomy. Femonationalism therefore operates from a cynical place, presenting itself as liberating Muslim women at the same time doing the exact opposite.

The Far Right and liberal politics should not be equated, since the former wants to have rights for a few, while the latter advocates for equality for all. Conservative women are not owners of feminism; they undermine them actively.

Far-right women's groups have upheld discriminatory movements targeting abortion. Article 218 defines abortion as murder in Germany, and Article 219a prohibits health care providers from advertising that they provide abortion services; these are Nazi-holdover decrees that have recently been softened but not abolished.

Anti-abortion activists in Poland have characterized the morning-after pill as an early-abortion pill, pressing for tighter abortion restrictions. Such accounts are not an exception but rather the traditional stance of femonationalism.

At the heart of these positions are European nativist concerns that they will be displaced by non-white European foreigners a trend embedded in legal and natalist policies since the early 2000's.

Under the Berlusconi government, in 2009 the Italian government introduced the Fondo Nuovi Nati (Fund for Newborns) to offer new mothers subsidized bank loans parents without Italian nationality were initially exempt from those benefits.

The Poland gives money to people to have more children, although it is unknown whether the universal child benefit can be extended to migrants. The ruling Law and Justice group, however, said it was weary for Muslim migrants to enjoy those benefits.

On the issue of large families, France's President Emmanuel Macron alleged that uneducated and African women had too many children, even though the French state has long provided subsidies to French parents that desire to have multiple children. These legal and stereotypical measures signal that not all forms of reproduction are equal.

Feminism history is full of traditions that left a few women behind. While Clara Zetkin and Rosa Luxemburg advocated full suffrage and political participation, German feminist Helene Stöcker advocated eugenics for Hebung der Rasse, or lifting up the white race. In the early and mid-20th centuries, the eugenics movement in the United States twisted with forced sterilization programs mostly targeting people with disabilities, women of color, working poor women; and sex workers.

The Dorothy Roberts provides ample archival evidence in her seminal text killing the Black Body about the way black women have been systematically sterilized in the United States. There was also sterilization of Puerto Rican and Native American women, beliefs of Aryan racial superiority serving as the fodder for these policies.

The collection of feminists which defended and continue to defend colonialism is even more egregious. More inclusive feminisms like the Combahee River group and post-colonial feminists have stepped in to counter sexism and patriarchal imaginations, but women in political-power positions across Europe definitely are not paying heed to them.

The challenge to Femonationalism in issue is not just a matter of moral posturing. Instead, it will mean stressing the ways in which anti-Muslim and anti-immigrant policies and rhetoric, whether implicit or explicit, have given the motivation to far right.

The increasing feminist international trend will pose a direct challenge. The authors uncover the last several years of political struggle to write in a slim manifesto by feminist scholars Cinzia Arruzza, Tithi Bhattacharya, and Nancy Fraser, standing for all who are exploited, dominated, and oppressed; it seeks to become a source of hope for the whole of mankind.

That is why one calls it 99% feminism. At the same time, the political check over the coming years is to create open and transparent demands to counter the rising far-right movement in Europe.

As a new generation of feminists and queers build, a movement that tackles housing, migration, health, and prison issues, feminism will have to separate itself specifically from nationalism. Since femonationalism has nothing to do with feminism, and with all to do with ethnic nationalism (Figure 7.4).

Figure 7.4: Feminist women protesting against violence.

Sources: Image by Pixabay.

7.7. CONCLUSION

There are large numbers of countries that have gain independence. The Woman gain equality by law by making of constitution. The Provisions of constitutions permitted the woman to leave the peaceful environment of their houses to take part in political sphere that is generally the male-dominated area though it has been very lower affair in the start.

Slowly the woman starts to raise voice against discrimination, and this threatens the status quo of society. The men in political positions started to feel threatened as it challenged their masculinity and their assumption that they have the right to rule.

In this Modern world, the VAW for taking part in politics has no place in society particularly in democracy. There is a need for strict laws to stop violence against woman for participating in politics.

There are many countries around the world that in theory are democratic, but the ground situations are different in these countries. The women in these countries mainly in Latin America, and south East Asia face threat of violence if they raise their voice against injustice or decide to take part in politics.

The Good news is that there is growing awareness in this direction and hopefully in future there be complete stop to VAW in politics.

REFERENCES

1. Align Platform, (n.d.). *Gender Norms and Women's Political Participation: Global Trends and Findings on Norm Change | Align Platform*. [online] Available at: https://www.alignplatform.org/resources/gender-norms-and-womens-political-participation-global-trends-and-findings-norm-change (accessed on 25 April 2020).
2. Bonhomme, E., (2019). *The Disturbing Rise of 'Femonationalism.'* [online] The Nation. Available at: https://www.thenation.com/article/archive/feminism-nationalism-right-eu (accessed on 25 April 2020).
3. Brechenmacher, S., (2020). *Fighting Violence Against Women in Politics: The Limits of Legal Reform*. [online] IPI Global Observatory. Available at: https://theglobalobservatory.org/2017/10/fighting-violence-against-women-in-politics-the-limits-of-legal-reform/#_ftnref11 (accessed on 25 April 2020).
4. Celis, K., Kantola, J., Waylen, G., & Weldon, S., (2013). *Introduction: Gender and Politics: A Gendered World, a Gendered Discipline*. Oxford Handbooks Online.
5. Restrepo, S. J., (2018). The law and violence against women in politics. *Politics and Gender, 14*(4), 676–680.

Chapter 8

Decriminalization of Politics

CONTENTS

The subject "decriminalization of politics" is assuming more and more relevance day by day. The need of cleansing politics of criminal influences is there, as transparency, accountability, prosperity, and good governance are compromised and sacrificed due to criminalization of politics.

The criminalization of politics is said to be done when criminals enter politics, contest elections and even get elected to the legislative bodies of the states. It takes place primarily due to nexus between the politicians and the criminals.

The criminals need the patronage of politicians to carry out their unlawful activities and politicians need the criminals to wield the muscle power and money, which criminals can offer them, to win elections.

This nexus between politicians and criminals has consequentially led to formulation of legal framework of criminal laws for decriminalization of politics. But the political process for legislation of ever-expanding criminal laws became counterproductive and detrimental to cleansing of governance.

Although there is no uniform remedy for decriminalization of politics, this subject is more relevant to democracies in developing nations, as each country has its own socio-political and socio-economic system.

But, here in this chapter we will dwell broadly upon the reasons of criminalization, various arguments against it, and various concepts and definitions of decriminalization, and various reforms in the political and legal processes to decriminalize the politics and make the political governance more transparent and accountable.

8.1. BACKGROUND: THE ROLE OF THE UN IN ADVOCATING DEMOCRACY AND THE EMERGENCE OF DEVELOPING NATIONS

After Second World War, ended United Nations Organization was established on 24 October 1945, with the intent to promote international cooperation. Its main objectives as per charter were:

- To maintain international peace and security.
- To develop friendly relations amongst nations on the basis of equality and the principle of self-determination. Initially, United Nations had 51 nations as its members.

Although the word 'democracy' in not mentioned explicitly in UN Charter, yet the opening words of its preamble "We the People" reflect the fundamental principle of democracy-that the will of the people is the source of legitimacy of sovereign states and therefore, of the UN as a whole.

The UN does not advocate for any specific model of the government, it promotes democratic governance as a set of values and principles that should be followed for greater participation, equality, security, and human development.

Democracy provides an environment that respects human rights and fundamental freedoms, and in which freely expressed will of the people is exercised. People have a say in decisions and can hold decision-makers accountable. Women and men have equal rights and all people are free from discrimination.

The Second World War had a very severe and adverse effect on the economies of European Nations, which were colonial powers in pre-Second World War period and had colonies all over the world, especially in Asia and Africa.

As a consequence of economic crisis faced by European nations, combined with formation of the UN, these colonies gained independence and with passing time emerged as underdeveloped and developing countries of the world. With emergence of developing and underdeveloped countries, the strength of members of the UN increased to 193 in 2011.

Decriminalization reflects changing social and moral views. A society may come to the view that an act is not harmful, should no longer be criminalized, or is otherwise not a matter to be addressed by the criminal justice system.

8.1.1. Developing Countries

The main characteristics of developing countries are low per capita income, high population growth rate, high rates of unemployment, lesser developed industrial base, and generally poor infrastructure.

These countries have higher health risks, energy crisis, low levels of education, widespread poverty, corruption at all government levels and lack of so-called good governance. All these factors lead to dissatisfaction of the general public, and their yearning for improvement in overall quality of life and good governance gives an edge to the criminals who are trying to enter politics for furthering their business, to enter the political system leading to criminalization of politics.

8.2. REASONS FOR CRIMINALIZATION OF POLITICS

Criminalization of politics has many forms, but the most alarming of all is:

1. A significant number of elected representatives are with criminal charges pending against them.
2. In the past decades, financing of elections had been an issue. Restrictions are imposed by governments on sources for funding the elections.
3. With passing of time, the cost of fighting elections has gone up and far above the legal spending limits. This has led to adoption of unfair means for managing expenses for election. Political parties field candidates with criminal background, because they do not have to worry about meeting their electoral expenses. Such candidates have money and muscle power.
4. Such candidates of criminal background sometimes have the support of general public, because public feels that they can get the work done and achieve the results with their muscle power. This results in lack of transparency, widespread corruption, and spread of illegal money.
5. When candidates with criminal background enter the state legislatures and parliament, they have a detrimental influence of law-making process, governance, expansion of criminal codes that expose the ordinary citizens to criminal punishments for innocuous Behavior and action.

- Criminalization of politics adversely affects the electoral process by means of:
- Booth capturing;
- Intimidation of voters;
- Tampering with electoral rolls;
- Large scale rigging of elections;
- Proliferation of non-serious candidates to divide the votes;

- Abuse of religion and caste in voter mobilization.

8.3. CONSEQUENCES OF CRIMINALIZATION OF POLITICS

As discussed earlier, the major impact of criminalization is that a lawbreaker becomes a lawmaker when he enters the parliament or state legislatures. This makes the parliament and legislative process less effective and efficient in enacting much needed and necessary laws meant for administration of the country.

As a consequence, the legislature loses its credibility and the council of ministers loses the legitimacy to administer and govern the country.

'Political patronage' of criminals aligned together with 'culture of adjournment' prevent the speedy trial of elected representatives, who have a criminal background or misuse their office. Added to this, the rule of criminal law, on which the criminal justice system is based, that an accused is treated as innocent, unless he is proved guilty.

Thus, in case the accused is convicted by the trial court and he appeals against it in the higher court, his conviction is suspended, till judgment on the appeal is pronounced and the accused becomes innocent again and is free to conduct himself in office and contest the elections, until proved guilty.

These issues make public prosecution ineffective and tainted by vested interests. Consequentially, it increases the circulation of illegal money during elections as well as after it, and also dilutes the probity in public life.

The increase of corruption in public life weakens the state institutions, the bureaucracy, the executive, the legislature, and the judiciary. Further, it may give rise to violence in society and sets a very bad precedence for the youth to follow. In many developing countries, it has led to overthrow of democratically elected governments and installation of authoritarian regimes.

8.4. THE NECESSITY FOR DECRIMINALIZATION OF POLITICS

Most of the developing and underdeveloped countries had been colonies of the European countries and had been exploited by them for their gain for two hundred years or more. Each developing nation has its own share of struggle for freedom from their respective colonial masters and thus the democracy was earned by them in a hard way.

The most significant characteristic for success of any democracy is election process, through which the people elect their representatives to govern their country. Therefore, for a good and effective democratic system free and fair electoral process is a must. In a healthy democracy, people have their say in the government and have allegiance and faith in the various democratic institutions of their country.

Therefore, in a nation with healthy democratic values, economic development takes place and peoples' aspirations are met and rule of law is there.

On the other hand, if electoral process is not free and fair, then there is lack of transparency in the system and democratic values are compromised. Corruption in the system prevails and economic development is retarded. People gradually lose faith in the democratic systems as their aspirations are not met.

The loss of peoples' faith in democracy has serious consequences:

- People with criminal background enter political arena of that country and often get elected to the country's legislature, thus becoming part of the government. This is because the people believe that politicians with criminal background can get the work done because of their strong-armed influence on the system.
- Failure of democratic system has led to overthrow of elected governments in developing and underdeveloped countries and installation of authoritarian regimes. In some cases, authoritarian governments may be good for economic developments but people's aspirations are not met and human rights are compromised. But mostly, this is not the case.

Therefore, highest legislative bodies of the countries have to make laws to ensure that free and fair elections are conducted, people with criminal background do not enter the election process, and elections are conducted by an independent body. It is also equally important, that the remedial measures are there in the system so that in case of any violation of law, the matter is adequately and timely addressed.

8.5. CRIMINALIZATION AND DECRIMINALIZATION: A CONCEPTUAL DISCUSSION

Each country has its own set of social, political, economic, and cultural characteristics, as manifested in their beliefs and aspirations. The policies and legal codes including criminal codes, framed for governance are customary and specific to that country. As such, there cannot be a single set legal codes or criminal laws and measures leading to criminalization and decriminalization in various spheres including politics.

However, criminalization and decriminalization of politics can be broadly discussed based on the works done and experiences of the USA and India, the two countries which have nothing in common, except that both are thriving democracies. Both countries have different political systems and have faced different issues. The USA is a developed nation whereas India is a developing nation.

8.5.1. Criminal Codes Expand But Don't Contract

The political process for legislation of criminal law can be called 'one-way route.' With passing time and experience, more additions are being done in criminal codes. The consequence of ever-expanding criminal laws that are meant to prevent crime is that it theoretically makes everyone look like a criminal.

Not only it makes a common man look like a criminal, it increases the discretionary powers of prosecuting authorities enormously, and with so many broad codes, they can pick and choose the offenders and offences alike. The result is aggravation of punishment because for same conduct there are multiple punishments under multiple criminal codes.

This phenomenon makes the criminal law incomprehensible to common public who face a variety of problems in complying with law in good faith. This undermines the legitimacy of criminal law.

It is also true, on the other hand, that State Legislatures have been narrowing or repealing criminal law provisions, reducing the severity of offence and modifying low level crimes to civil violation of rules.

There have also been many instances, where state legislatures have refused to pass the proposed new expanded criminal laws, include many that seemed politically irresistible on standard accounts. Thus, state legislatures have played the role of both expanding and narrowing the criminal laws.

Sometimes, the interest groups and popular public opinion support and drive decriminalization, when legislatures, in fact, criminalize small conducts which in public opinion need not be guided by law. Law Commissions appointed by legislatures or governments, which comprise of experts, also drive the legal reforms and odds of their success increase, when driven by special procedural mechanisms.

In addition, when the redundant and out dated crimes and criminal laws pertaining to these, are ignored during reforms and continue to appear in law books, the other components of the democratic governance come into the play and compensate for same: the prosecutors who are accountable politically in fact, rarely take action, and many crimes that are not significant or relevant are nullified.

It is obvious that criminalization of politics is more perverse in nature. Most criminalization of wholly innocent conduct is either found in federal law, where the argument for nonfunctioning politics of crime is strong or constitutes of petty offences that are never enforced by enforcing authorities.

8.6. OVERCRIMINALIZATION

The growth of criminal codes over a period of time leads to overcriminalization. One of the reasons for overcriminalization is increase in nature and types of crimes with advancement in technologies. Two decades ago, cybercrime was an unknown phenomenon.

The codes of criminal laws have increased universally to adjust with the change of circumstances and increase in nature of crimes, which was necessary. But the other side of this expansion, the criminal law has its own share of disadvantages, which are detrimental in nature and have adverse effect on the entire socio-political and socio-economic systems, as follows:

8.6.1. Redundancy

It means that there are multiple statutes for the similar types of conduct, carrying different and varying punishments. Redundancy does not expand the scope of criminal law. It recriminalizes the conduct, which is already prohibited by law.

8.6.2. Overbreadth

Certain criminal codes over expand to accommodate various crimes and thus tend to criminalize the conduct of most people, which are innocuous, innocent, or very small in nature. Thus, overbreadth inappropriately criminalizes normally legitimate conduct, infringing the liberty granted by the constitution.

8.6.3. Disorganization of Codes

Expansion of criminal law leads to addition of new provisions throughout the law books outside legal codes. Such addition of new provisions in law books in a scattered manner leads to incoherence and their inconsistent application, where similar or comparable misconducts yield different sentences.

The application of criminal law is relegated to police, prosecutors, counsels, and judges, who are principal actors in the criminal justice system, in order to regulate the conduct of the people. This phenomenon results into a number of problems for the people who are trying to comply with the law in good faith. Overcriminalization makes it extremely difficult for common persons to understand where the line of criminality lies.

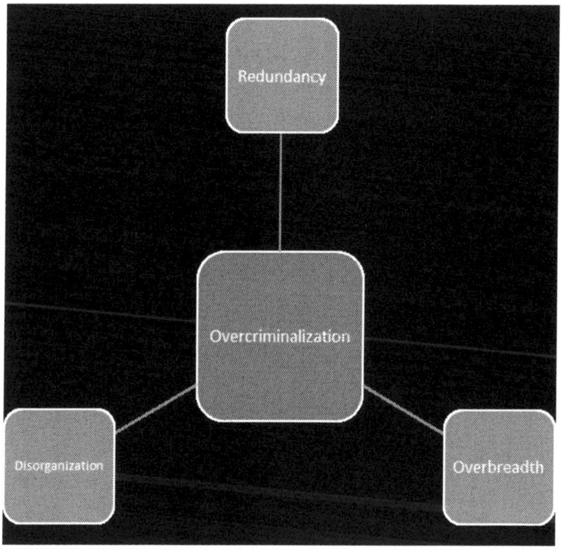

Figure 8.1: Various adverse impacts of overcriminalization.

They empower the prosecutors to impose various and arbitrary charges for the same conduct, under various similar legal statutes having easy proof requirements. And they coerce the parties to plead guilty by threatening them to impose varying provisions resulting in higher sentences, when case goes on trial. After the case goes on trial, it is left to judiciary to decide whether the law was broken or not. Courts, on the other hand, have fewer means to control the prosecutors' manipulation of charging options, created by overlapping offences, through concurrent sentencing, merging offences and rules mandating that specific statutes supersede general ones (Figure 8.1).

8.7. LIMITATION OF THE LEGISLATURE

Legislatures have a very limited or no option in addressing issues of criminal justice. They cannot get directly involved in decisions in specific cases.

In fact, to curb the crime rate, legislatures can pass legislations and approve budgets of law enforcement agencies, but these efforts have their own limitations. Only through the legislations creating new crimes, increasing sentences for offences already on the books and reducing procedural and evidence requirements on the police and prosecutors, a legislator can have a direct effect on the crime.

Even authoritarian regimes have limited political parties, interest groups and legislatures. Elections are held for these legislatures with participations from political parties in a limited way, but here the elected representatives do not represent the people's will. Rather, such legislatures provide political legitimacy to the authoritarian governments.

8.8. CRIMINALIZATION ARGUMENTS

There are basically three types of arguments for and against the use of criminal law.

- Arguments of principle assert that as a matter of political or moral thinking, it may be proper or improper to prohibit a certain conduct.
- **Arguments of Practicality:** These are of relevance logically, only if it has been ascertained that the society may legitimately prohibit certain conducts in question; and practical discussions assert that though prohibitions of certain conduct are legitimate, but they will do more harm than good, if put into practice.
- The third argument rejects the feasibility of devising a workable standard based on substance of prohibitions and calls for

additional procedural limitations on criminalization decisions and criminal law enforcement.

8.8.1. Arguments of Principle

The discussion on the issue that to what extent morality may be enforced legally, tend to focus on the use of formal criminal sanctions and most of the reasons given do not make any distinction between criminal and non-criminal measures. In this case, if legal intervention is there for certain type of conduct, then the question arises that whether it is legitimate, necessary, or desirable to use criminal sanctions.

8.8.1.1. Principled Arguments Favoring Prohibition

Some experts say that the society is allowed, or even has an obligation to enforce morality either through criminal or legal sanctions. However, experts have two distinct variations of these arguments. While some assert that, the majority in the society have the right not only to follow and preserve their own moral convictions, but insist that all members of the society should abide by their moral convictions.

On the other hand, some experts argue that the law must protect society's political and moral institutions and "community of ideas" necessary for people to live together. However, even if legitimacy of legal enforcement of morality is agreed to, there are practical difficulties as to whose morality is to be enforced and to what extent.

Experts concede that the criminal law should be applied to extreme cases of gross acts of vice that are condemned by public opinion and common practices. Also, there is a need 'for toleration of maximum individual freedom that is consistent with integrity of the society'; only if the majority 'has a real feeling of reprobation, intolerance, indignation, and disgust' may it be prohibited.

8.8.1.2. Principled Arguments Against Criminalization

Proponents of decriminalization argue that criminal law may not prohibit legitimately, certain types of Behavior and society can intervene in the individual's freedom of action only to the extent that it does not cause any harm to the others. Individual liberty must be protected and individual must be accorded maximum level of autonomy, in consistency with the rights of the other people.

The experts against criminalization argue that the freedom and self-determination are the most important rights of an individual and should be given priority over mere considerations of the greater good for the majority.

The Apex Court and some state courts have favored this approach and upheld the rights of privacy and free expression of individuals totally in various amendments to prevent the state from prohibiting certain acts that do not cause any harm or injury directly to other person.

The apex court has also upheld that ban on some cruel and unusual type of punishments and principles of due protection, under certain set of situations prevent the criminal liability for moral or regulatory offences. On the other hand, the apex court has also mentioned that legislative judgments regarding prohibition of certain types of conduct, even if these judgments are made based on moral issues, should be broadly respected.

Some experts, however, do not share the view of total opposition to prohibitions for protecting the defendant's physical well-being. The argument of not prohibiting individuals' freedom of action, to the extent of not causing harm to others has raised the question that to what extent tangible and intangible harms can be differentiated.

8.8.2. Arguments of Practicality

Some experts in support of decriminalization have gone a step further by putting forth the argument that it may not be a wise action to invoke certain type of prohibitions though they are legitimate. Some writers have the view that the legal provisions regarding "victimless crimes" should be done away with.

Another set of experts call for making a catalog, enlisting the pros and cons of attempting to prohibit certain type of Behavior, and advocate cost-benefit analysis of criminalization.

Victimless Crime

The term "victimless crime" is misleading somewhat, though some experts suggest it as the basis of decriminalization. Whether this argument is viewed as an "argument of principle" or argument of practicality, this concept has very less applicability and utility in deciding difficult cases of criminalization.

This concept had been applied to offenses like public drunkenness and adultery which, often in most of the cases have direct victims who can readily be identified, hence considered vague and misleading.

Further, it has also been argued that other so-called victimless crimes, such as drug abuse, prostitution, etc. also have potential victims, easily identifiable in most of the cases like relatives, taxpayers, and offenders themselves.

Those who use this term also lay stress on practical difficulties in trying to enforce the victimless crimes. In such cases, lack of witnesses and complainants gives police a freehand to use intrusive practices, bribery, and forceful discriminatory enforcement of crime.

However, these type of issues of intrusive police practices also arise in enforcing the criminal laws on conducts, which are not labeled as victimless, or which are proposed for repealing. The criterion of victimless crime is vague in nature and cannot be defined clearly. It fails to cover some of the criminal acts to which it is applied and vice versa applies well on crimes that have not been proposed to be done away with.

The victimless crime can at the most be termed as a subjective, and related to several important practical issues, based on which it can be applied. The process of labeling a crime as victimless begins a very difficult process of assessment of complex facts and fundamental value choices.

The Cost-Benefit Approach

This approach to question of criminalization, seeks to identify and analyze specific advantages and disadvantages of invoking a criminal law for a particular type of conduct (Figure 8.2).

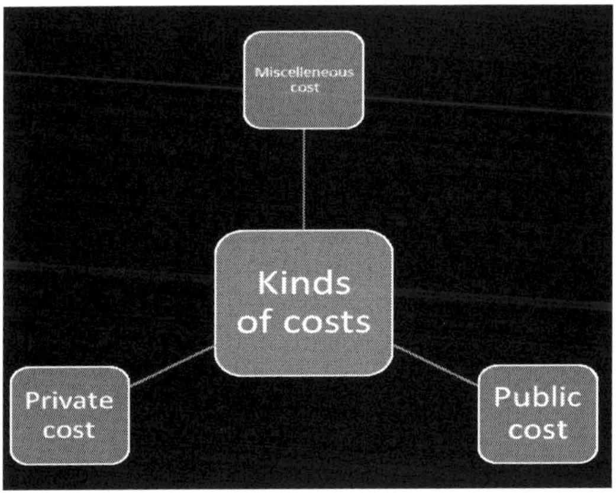

Figure 8.2: Different kinds of costs of criminalization.

It makes an effort to assess and determine whether the total cost of criminalization, including public and private cost is more or less than the benefits derived out of it. The cost-benefit analysis of variables that are measurable is made in monetary terms and other quantitative units.

Advocates of cost-benefit approach feel that this is a useful way of tackling the criminalization problems, although they agree that the quantitative data available for it quite less. The cost of criminalization comprises of both public and private costs, which may be tangible or intangible in nature.

1. **Public Cost of Criminalization:** For assessing tangible public cost, the cost of police, counsels, court, and correctional expenditures pertaining to particular criminal law needs to be separated, although it is almost clear and relevant data is available, like salaries, etc. In some cases, the apparent cost may not necessarily be separated with decriminalization.

Moreover, it is quite possible that decriminalization may need the intervention of police and other officials to the underlying behavioral problems in other ways that carry their own cost. For example, doing away with penalties for public drunkenness may entail further costs like increase in use of medical facilities or making more arrests for disorderly conduct.

2. **Private Cost of Criminalization:** These include measurable items like fees of the attorney and other litigation expenses. However, there are intangible costs that are hard to measure, such as loss of freedom, anxiety, social boycott or ostracism (whether or not the offender is caught and prosecuted), total or partial loss of earning (for the period of trial or sentence or for entire life), cost of detention and uncompensated costs of inconveniences that are imposed on witnesses and own families of offenders.
3. **Miscellaneous Costs of Criminalization:** These may affect both public as well as private interests and are briefly as mentioned below:

- Criminalization tends to produce more, rather than less socially undesirable Behavior, like bribery, extortion by officials for non-enforcement of law, blackmail, or threats to expose the offender.
- Discriminatory enforcement of law against select unpopular or opposing groups.
- Discriminatory enforcement of law may also be done in favor of offender or defendants who have more political, economic, or social muscle.
- Use of illegal methods to obtain evidence like electronic

surveillance, unauthorized searches, coercive interrogation and entrapment.

Some legal experts feel that certain category of crimes e.g., vagrancy, and disorderly conduct, has been designed specifically to undermine constitutional limitations on arrest, search, and interrogation.

8.9. WHAT IS DECRIMINALIZATION: MEANING AND DEFINITIONS

Although the meaning of word decriminalization seems to be very simple and self-explanatory, but as per the policy documents and legal literature, it has been defined and conceived in different ways that are sometimes very vague and inconsistent.

Decriminalization in itself covers multiple types of areas and activities, because of its encompassing nature and it has been very well explained by some experts in relation to its opposite concept, i.e., criminalization.

Thus, it is not a matter of surprise that the terms criminalization and decriminalization have been used to explain a number of legal and social situations in ways that sometimes they appear to be incohesive and confusing.

The assumptions, ideologies, intentions, and interests that are behind criminal legislations or the political promises underlying these legislations; those which make the common people aware of the decision-making process, along with patterns of policing and prosecution.

Added to above, outlines of criminal law doctrine, criminal law legislation, the practices followed by judiciary in application of criminal laws to particular offenders and handing out sentences to them; the practices by officials in the penal system; even the impact of social attitudes, economic costs, etc. and social effects followed by punishment; all these contribute to one's understanding of political and social phenomenon of criminalization.

Therefore, the concept of decriminalization may theoretically nullify and gobble up each and every question about criminal law, criminal responsibility, criminal justice, and punishment.

There are several references to decriminalization that are also used by UN Human Rights bodies in an inconsistent manner, leveraging on its legal definitions and its broader social conceptualizations.

These treaty bodies consider the issue of inadequate and inappropriate criminalization laws from a more legalistic view as they adjudicate individual communications and issue conclusive observations on state party's compliance with human rights treaties.

The independent experts and groups that operate under the Special Procedures of the Human Rights Council, consider the issue of decriminalization from a perspective that goes beyond the legal bounds, when they give thematic attention to issues of human rights.

Thus, obviously, the social accounts of criminalization are also examined by these bodies, as to how these are practiced, by whom, and against whom and what are the consequences of such criminalization practices. Then these are reviewed periodically for compliance on human rights obligations. Through this system, efforts are made to ensure equal scrutiny of all member states of the UN.

With such intricacies involved on the issue of decriminalization, it becomes necessary to go through the various terms and conceptions that collective UN human rights bodies put into use.

8.9.1. Legal Conceptions and Definitions

Decriminalization can be defined in formal terms as de jure decriminalization, de facto decriminalization or partial decriminalization. In de jure criminalization, legislatures do away with, or narrow down the criminal codes, to remove a conduct wholly or partly from the scope of criminal law.

This is often a codification of de facto practices of decriminalization, where an offence continues to appear in criminal codes but is not enforced. De facto decriminalization is due to fact that certain criminal statutes become obsolete and legally outdated and sometimes, it is considered less politically divisive and easier option not to invoke or enforce such criminal laws, rather than deleting them from the criminal codes.

Partial decriminalization refers to removal of all punishments while retaining the formal prohibition of conduct within the criminal codes. The partial decriminalization reflects the policy of continued disapproval by state and prohibition officially, with efforts accompanied to prevent or restrict the conduct, using the criminal, civil, or other provisions and implementation of programming targeted to reduce this type of misconduct.

Depenalization

Depenalization is another concept, in which custodial or jail sentences are reduced, in favor of other punitive or reformative measures, such as probation or some rehabilitation program, which is compulsory for this offense.

However, in such cases, the conduct for which custodial sentence is awarded continues to remain a criminal offense. Thus, depenalization is an entirely different and much narrower concept than decriminalization.

On the other hand, the concept of decriminalization sometimes extends beyond the criminal laws and applied to other legal areas for example imposition of administrative fines. This is in order to punish and prevent the misconduct for violation of laws, so that an individual is not drawn into criminal justice system.

Nonpayments of administrative fines may result in other penalties like various administrative restrictions and social incarceration. Such regulatory and administrative measures are sometimes equally strict.

Legalization

Legalization is another term which is entirely different from decriminalization. It can be used and described in two ways. Firstly, it refers to the conducts and actions, that are forbidden or prohibited by practice, are permitted by law and the individual is allowed to follow or use them.

Secondly, it means or refers to transferring the control of an action or conduct to the legal system, or in simple terms the policy or practice of regulating the conduct that has been decriminalized, to the legal system. The examples of such practices are public health regulations, licensing, etc.

8.9.2. Socio-Legal Conceptions and Definitions

Socio-legal conceptions scrutinize the decriminalization not only within entire criminal justice system. They are used to examine broader political and social processes, of which criminal justice system is a part, internally as well as internationally.

Socio-legal conceptions help one to understand that under which circumstances and with what consequences, how legal categories and their provisions are applied and to whom they can be applied.

They enable the examination of "the relations of class, race, and gender, the cultural assumptions and prejudices, and the political considerations that inform and influence the practice of law," and the "partial targeted, and often in discriminatory ways" in which the criminal laws are applied.

The conceptual framework of criminalization propounded by Nicola Lacey can be used to understand the socio-legal approach of UN human rights bodies, to the issue of decriminalization. Criminalization may take place as a practice or as an outcome and both of which have a factual & meaningful and formal component.

What has been criminalized and what should be criminalized formally through decisions of legislature, prosecutor or judiciary, or what has and should be criminalized meaningfully, through actual implementation of these formal norms fall under the category of criminalization as an outcome.

On what assumptions the formal or substantive criminalization has been done, who does it, and according to what principles and what processes, the criminalization has been done is known as criminalization by practice.

UN human rights bodies go beyond the normative and legal aspects to review the issue of decriminalization. The UN human rights bodies not only review whether the content and scope of criminal law is consistent with international human rights norms, but are also consistent with the policy, structural, and practical considerations of decriminalization.

They also look into the process and see how the application of criminal laws affects an individual, or a particular group or the society as a whole, in which the criminal justice system is embedded.

The UN human rights bodies also examine the application of criminal laws, which may become more intense or may diminish, depending upon the process by which they are evolved, how they are disseminated, operationalized, and implemented. This may depend upon the available resources, penal politics, media coverage, etc. that inform the ways and means by which the prosecutors exercise their discretionary powers.

8.10. REMEDIES TO PREVENT CRIMINALIZATION OF POLITICS

Earlier in this chapter, we have discussed the characteristics of developing countries, and why decriminalization of politics is relevant for success of democracy in these countries.

Before deliberating further on the issue of decriminalization of politics, let us briefly cite the case of the Indian Sub-continent. Indian subcontinent gained independence in 1947 and two countries India and Pakistan came into existence. Democratic governments were installed in both the countries. Both the countries suffered with issues of corruption, economic development, etc.

While in Pakistan, democratically elected government was overthrown by army within 12 years, democracy thrived in India in spite of its issues of development, corruption in public life and gradual criminalization of political system.

This is because the political leadership of India had the will to preserve its democratic institutions and there were regular and continuous efforts to evolve and implement electoral reforms and relook and pass and enforce the legislations to decriminalize the system.

Based on the experiences in India, the most populous democratic country, the following remedies can be broadly seen as the measures to decriminalize the political system in democratic developing countries (Figure 8.3).

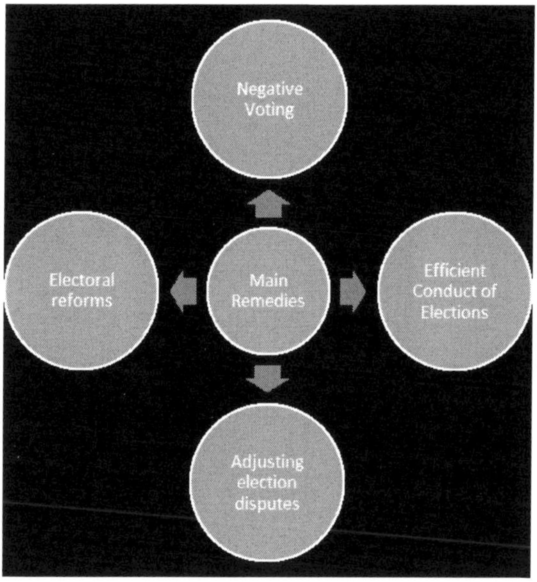

Figure 8.3: Four main remedies to decriminalize politics.

8.10.1. Negative Voting

As a result of rampant corruption in the system, infiltration of people with criminal background in politics, use of intimidating tactics to frighten the voters and use of violence, etc., the honest and committed people may avoid contesting the elections in one or more constituencies.

As a result, such constituencies witness low voter turnout by fear or due to loss of desire to be a part of election process. This results in same candidate, whether incompetent or with criminal background or both, getting elected again and again to the legislature. The election conducting body and legal committees constituted, reiterate the system of neutral or negative voting. In this system, the voters have a choice to reject the candidates on ballot by selecting 'none of the above option.' With this system, there is a possibility to democratic safeguard through proportional share of negative votes.

In such a case, if sufficient neutral votes are polled, there is a possibility of election being declared null and void and taking up of re-election in that constituency.

8.10.2. Efficient Management of Conducting Elections

This can be achieved by prevention of rigging of elections, which has become a common feature of elections in developing countries. The first step of an electoral process in preparation of electoral rolls.

Influential persons or sometimes political parties enable and manage registration of bogus voters on a large scale or deletion of unfriendly voters from electoral rolls. The situation is made worse by election officials who collaborate with the dishonest and criminal candidates for their own vested interests or out of fear, to do the tampering with the election process.

This issue can be addressed by creation of online database of voters by election body. It calls for each legitimate voter possessing a voter card with unique bar code which can be easily verified at the polling booth by a handheld device.

However, this suggestion can be undermined with physical intimidation of voters. To mitigate this problem the election conducting body should be given powers to cancel the elections and call for a fresh election.

8.10.3. Adjudication of Election Disputes

Disputes related to elections of the State Legislatures and Union Legislature is dealt by High Courts. Law provides that the court shall make all out efforts to dispose of the election petitions within a period of six months from the date of admission of case. Also, as far as possible the hearings should be held every day to complete it within stipulated period.

However, cases involving elections are very rarely closed with the desired time frame and remain pending for years together. Sometimes, the full term of the house expires and election petitions lose their sanctity and become infructuous.

8.10.4. Electoral Reforms

Reform is a continuous process. However, the compliance and implementation of reforms requires coordination of electoral machinery, political parties, administrative machinery, candidates, and electorate at all the levels. The election conducting bodies or election commission of a state can be a driver to handle a number of issues and accomplish number of electoral reforms to strengthen the democracy and ensure fairness of elections.

These changes made by the Election Commission of India are significant and commendable and can be the guiding force for other developing countries, though they may have their own systems.

The judiciary also has its own share in guiding electoral reforms. In one of the cases, Apex Court of a State acknowledged the damaging impact of the criminals on the political system. It called upon Head of the State to set up a high-level committee, in consultation with Prime Minister and Speaker of the parliament, to look upon and recommend measures to eliminate the nexus between criminals, politicians, and bureaucrats.

8.10.5. More Suggestive Measures

The criminalization of politics is a deep-rooted problem in developing countries and over the years has permeated the very core of the political system as well as public life. Hence, creation of a new independent body or a nodal agency for implementation of systems cannot be expected to address the eradication of all malpractices prevailing in the system.

Although, the existing institutions in some of the developing nations, like election commission in India, have over the years strived and had been instrumental in implementing the commendable electoral reforms, yet it has not been successful entirely, and maladies in the system are still prevalent.

There are two main reasons, firstly the election conducting bodies do not have sweeping powers and needs government intervention through the entire electoral process, including maintaining law and order during polling. Secondly, as a consequence, the election conducting bodies have been unable to function as a cohesive unit.

Therefore, multi-pronged approach is need of the hour to prevent decriminalization of politics. All components of the system beginning with legislature, government, judiciary, pressure groups, media, up to citizens have to play their roles positively to achieve a healthy political system, free from corruption and criminals.

The legislature in itself should create a system by enacting reforms to root out the evil from within it and giving effective powers to election conducting body to control the elections effectively.

The government machinery needs to be restructured, so as to weed out the criminal elements within the entire system. Arming of election conducting bodies with overriding powers to conduct free and fair polls is the requirement of the day.

Empowerment of citizens by law of the land is also a solution, in which the citizens can act upon their own against intimidation, clan, caste, and regional considerations and vote for the right person. Positive political culture is need of the day, so that the citizens have the power to influence the events, resources, and human Behavior to guide and control the system.

Nowadays, independent electronic media, social media, and internet carry tremendous weight and can exercise their positive influence on the system. However, the present political system in most of the developing countries is such that it inhibits the positive influence of its people and favors the existing political parties and concerned individuals.

Many promising individuals in field of politics, lose their interest or go into oblivion as they do not have support and backing of big political parties.

Hence, active participation by the people at grass roots level, whether backed by any political party or not, is required. The gradual rise of good people from grass roots level into the system can bring positive changes within leading to decriminalization of the system to a great extent.

Although electoral reforms, legislature, and judiciary have a limited role to play, effective legislations of criminal law prescribing harsh punishments for vandalizing the electoral and political system, may serve as a deterrent, as can be seen from the experience of majority of the countries.

With large portion of electorate being illiterate in many developing countries, accompanied by poverty, it is a herculean task to imbibe a sense of political thinking in them. Such citizens bear the brunt of criminal activities and injustice from their elected representatives.

Large structural changes are required in the systems for development as well as cleansing of the system. The onus of providing good governance to their countries is now going to be on politicians and political parties, who can exhibit and demonstrate that they can offer governance, without necessarily being self-serving or being totally cold and heartless while their interactions with public.

There have been political leaders in developing countries like India, who have worked towards civil services reforms, cleaning up of system, clipping the discretionary powers of the states and regulating the businesses, so that they cannot expand to extent to monopolize the system, resulting in one man show.

However, unfortunately all these changes have come due to surfacing of big scandals that have had adverse effect on the economy many common citizens have been hurt. It is a cold fact in political circles that it is the crisis that leads to the reforms.

An honest person, who has a keen interest in public service, today makes a critical assessment of his future, before deciding to enter domain of public service, because he does want to associate himself with a profession which is dominated by ruffians and criminals. Such people are at crossroads, where instead of creating good systems and being a change agent for good, they plunge into the gutter of corruption and crime.

This weakness of the legal systems in most developing and underdeveloped countries is advantageous to the criminals. Firstly, they can escape law of the land with engaging in illegal activities and there is rare chance of them getting caught and face the justice.

Second implication is that once such criminal elements get elected to the office, they can get the things done that allows them to manipulate and bend the rules in their favor, to favor the people or groups supporting them.

Such politicians with criminal background have a negative influence on the system, especially the police to help the people who help them for their misdeeds.

This vicious of nexus between politicians and criminals starts from the periphery of the politics, when at the time of elections, the criminals become active as agents of candidates in election fray to mobilize or suppress the voter turnout, or hand out goodies to the poor voters, in favor of their candidates.

Over a period of time, these criminals become influential and enter the political arena as candidates of the political parties in elections, for whom they have worked. These criminal elements are quite resourceful and are there on their own, as they do not need any funding from parties for contesting the elections.

This is how illegal money acquired through illegal sources is used for fighting elections. These criminal elements also have an edge, as they know how the illegal money in large amounts can be moved in the political system, without it getting detected.

It is also seen that voters who are well aware about the candidates, often support and vote for candidates with criminal background, contrary to the common wisdom that awareness leads to making of right choices.

This is due to the fact that in democracies where democratically elected is considered weak and corruption is there and government is not considered impartial, there is a tendency to find someone who can fill the gap and deliver the results.

The candidates with criminal background, perceiving this as a sign of their credibility, use their muscle power to get the work done for their constituents. The identity of candidates on religious, caste or ethnic lines also plays a very important role in election of candidates with criminal background leading to criminalization of politics.

8.10.6. The Role of Election Conducting Institutions or Election Commissions

The election commission of a country has to formulate and enforce a model code of conduct on candidates contesting the elections, to keep a check on them and their campaigning activities. The candidates can be asked:

- To disclose their criminal antecedents in their affidavit, in order to inform the citizens regarding their criminal background and cases pending against them.
- To voluntary disclose their assets as well as the assets of their family members. This provides a means to judge honesty and integrity of the candidates.

Further, there has to be a mechanism in place to monitor the expenses made by a candidate to contest the elections and to scrutinize the source from which the money has been arranged.

8.10.7. Negative Vote

As discussed, an earlier option for negative vote in the ballot for voters can also be a means to reject voters with criminal backgrounds. This is a means to show the political parties in election fray that the citizens have the option of not electing a criminal to power, because all political parties have a notorious track record of fielding criminals in the elections. The election commissions should have absolute independence and autonomy in financial matters, as well as recommend the various laws to the governments, to bring about decriminalization in political systems. For example, debarring a candidate charged with serious criminal offenses from contesting elections.

8.10.8. Role of Media

With technological advancement and advent of internet, media has a very powerful and effective role to play in decriminalization of political system. Right referred as "Fourth Pillar of Democracy," media in past has played a very significant role in the process of decriminalization and had conducted several sting operations to expose the corrupt acts of the politicians.

Election Commissions had relied on media to make the public aware on educational, financial, and criminal background of the contestants fighting the elections. By publishing the studies on extent of criminalization of politics and supporting them, media not only attracts the public attention but also exerts pressure on the governments to take corrective actions.

Electronic media operating 24×7 with multiple news channels all over the world, the wrongful acts of politicians come into public domain immediately, has increased the level of awareness of the public multi-fold.

Often it is alleged that either media houses are controlled by the governments or by politicians, it is a bare fact that the consistent efforts of media and its various components, that common men can make their concern heard on criminalization of politics.

Social media has also become a very powerful medium for the people to voice their concerns and generate a mass movement by building up a public opinion on various issues including infestation of criminals in political systems.

In various social media like Facebook, WhatsApp, and Twitter people can connect with each other, discuss, and voice their concerns and generate a collective opinion to put pressure on the government.

But on the negative side, the social media can be used to spread a canard or rumors, which can sometimes assume dangerous proportions detrimental to law and order. Hence, social media needs to be somewhat controlled or regulated, so that it can be used wisely and effectively in a positive manner.

8.11. CHALLENGES TO DECRIMINALIZATION OF POLITICS

Even after combined and concerted efforts from all sides including the government, the legislature, the judiciary, election commission, and public, the wait for decriminalization of politics looks longer and longer. Various recommendations in this regard need to be implemented and the people, who have the authority to execute and implement these, are a part of the problem.

The election commissions appointed by governments have limited powers. Judiciary, time, and again has refrained from taking concrete action and has directed legislatures to make policies to mitigate the problems. The legislators who belong to one or political parties, do not have the will to enact a reform, because they are the part of the problem and want the problem to remain in place to serve their own ends.

The recent judgment made by the apex court of a nation can become a hallmark towards decriminalization of political system, as it puts the responsibility of decriminalization directly on political parties. It is seen as a crucial step towards removing tainted politicians with criminal background, insulated from justice just by virtue of being members of the legislature.

It puts the onus of listing out all criminal cases pending against a candidate on the political parties. Moreover, the political parties have to upload and publish these details on their website and social media accounts.

The most embarrassing part of the order is that the political parties are required to put an explanation on the reasons for fielding a candidate with criminal cases, rather than selecting an honest candidate with sound integrity and clean background.

By not complying with order, political parties may face contempt of court, which is a punishable offence. All political parties extensively use the platform of social media to canvass for their promotional programs and candidates and on the other hand to malign their opponents. Hence, they cannot afford to make any mistake of concealing the facts, as it may result in trolling of public figures by people.

The only argument on the negative side of this judgment is that all political parties have fielded candidates with criminal background and allowed them to climb higher in the system. So, it is a catch-22 situation for all political parties and no one is the winner. None of the parties is clean and this is a threat to effectiveness of this judgment.

However, the awareness level of the voters is much higher than before. Although the political parties may avoid discussions on the matter and shy away from raising fingers at each other, being on the same side of the coin, the voters armed with information about their candidates will make a conscious choice instead of going by rhetoric of political parties.

Although the process of decriminalization is slow and it may take time for change to come, the political parties are well aware of the fact that the electorate is no more gullible now and judiciary is watching them closely.

8.12. CONCLUSION

When criminals enter the political system and manage to get elected to legislature and become part of the government, economic growth gets retarded, democratic institutions are compromised and people lose faith in the democratic processes.

A number of measures have been taken for decriminalization of politics, starting from electoral reforms like giving electorate the choice 'none of the above' i.e., negative voting, streamlining the electoral rolls by election conducting body. A number of rulings have also been given by the apex courts like declaration of criminal cases against candidates and their publication on website of political parties.

However, one single institution like election conducting body or election commission, or legislature or judiciary cannot decriminalize the politics. The process of decriminalization of politics is painfully slow. Holistic decriminalization of politics can only be achieved by adopting multipronged approach, in which each and every component of the system has to function.

The legislature, the judiciary, the election commission, the media and above all the citizens have to play their role proactively and positively. In the age of internet when information is readily available and public awareness is ever-increasing, there is a hope that with more and more transparency, the political system will get rid of the criminals.

REFERENCES

1. Beniwal, N., (n.d.). *Electoral Reforms Towards Decriminalizing Politics*. [online] Legalservicesindia.com. Available at: http://www.legalservicesindia.com/article/1614/Electoral-Reforms-Towards-Decriminalizing-Politics.html (accessed on 25 April 2020).
2. Brown, D., (2006). *Democracy and Decriminalization*. [eBook] Available at: https://www.researchgate.net/publication/228249441_Democracy_and_Decriminalization (accessed on 25 April 2020).
3. Career Launcher, (2019). *Criminalization of Politics: Remedies to Prevent the Criminalization of Politics > Career Launcher*. [online] Available at: https://www.careerlauncher.com/blogs/criminalization-of-politics-remedies-to-prevent-the-criminalization-of-politics/ (accessed on 25 April 2020).
4. IASToppers. (2018). *Criminalization of Politics in India [Mains Article] | Iastoppers*. [online] Available at: https://www.iastoppers.com/criminalization-of-politics-in-india-mains-article/ (accessed on 25 April 2020).
5. Keehn, E., (2018). *Decriminalization and the U.N. Human Rights Bodies*. [eBook] Available at: https://hrp.law.harvard.edu/wp-content/uploads/2018/03/Emily-Keehn_HRP-18_002.pdf (accessed on 25 April 2020).
6. Larkin, J., (2011). *Overcriminalization: The Legislative Side of the Problem*. [online] The Heritage Foundation. Available at: https://www.heritage.org/crime-and-justice/report/overcriminalization-the-legislative-side-the-problem (accessed on 25 April 2020).
7. Law.jrank.org. (n.d.). *Criminalization and Decriminalization: A Review and Typology of Criminalization Arguments*. [online] Available at: https://law.jrank.org/pages/838/Criminalization-Decriminalization-review-typology-criminalization-arguments.html (accessed on 25 April 2020).
8. Peeyush, P., (2020). *Decriminalization of Politics: Supreme Court Order Puts Political Parties in a Catch-22 Situation*. [online] The Financial Express. Available at: https://www.financialexpress.com/india-news/decriminalisation-of-politics-supreme-court-order-puts-political-parties-in-a-catch-22-situation/1866786/ (accessed on 25 April 2020).
9. Un.org. (n.d.). *Democracy*. [online] Available at: https://www.un.org/

en/sections/issues-depth/democracy/index.html (accessed on 25 April 2020).

10. UPSCBUDDY, (2019). *Decriminalization of Politics: Where We Stand!* [online] Available at: https://upscbuddy.com/decriminalization-of-politics/ (accessed on 25 April 2020).
11. Vaishnav, M., (2017). *Does Democracy Encourage Criminal Politicians? Knowledge@Wharton.* [online] Knowledge@Wharton. Available at: https://knowledge.wharton.upenn.edu/article/does-democracy-encourage-criminal-politicians/ (accessed on 25 April 2020).

INDEX